THE FIVE RITUALS OF WEALTH

THE FIVE RITUALS OF
WEALTH

PROVEN STRATEGIES FOR TURNING
THE LITTLE YOU HAVE
INTO MORE THAN ENOUGH

TOD BARNHART

FOREWORD BY ANTHONY ROBBINS, AUTHOR OF *AWAKEN THE GIANT WITHIN*

HarperBusiness
A Division of HarperCollinsPublishers

This book is sold with the understanding that neither the author nor the publisher is engaged in rendering legal, accounting, or financial services. As each financial situation is unique, questions relevant to the practice of law, accounting, or personal finance and specific to the individual should be addressed to an appropriate professional for proper evaluation and advice.

The author and publisher specifically disclaim any liability, loss, or risk, personal or otherwise, which is incurred as a consequence, directly or indirectly, of the use and application of any of the contents of this work.

HarperCollins books may be purchased for educational, business, or sales promotional use. For information please write: Special Markets Department, HarperCollins Publishers, Inc., 10 East 53rd Street, New York, NY 10022.

FIRST EDITION

DESIGNED BY JOEL AVIROM & JASON SNYDER

Library of Congress Cataloging-in-Publication Data

Barnhart, Tod, 1967–
    The 5 rituals of wealth / by Tod Barnhart. — 1st ed.
        p.   cm.
    ISBN 0-88730-733-7
      1. Finance, Personal. 2. Wealth. I. Title. II. Title: Five rituals of wealth.
HG179.B333   1995
332.024'01—dc20   94-48462

95 96 97 98 99 ❖/RRD 10 9 8 7 6 5 4 3 2 1

To Cindy, my soul mate;
Mom, who taught me compassion and confidence;
Dad, who never gave up on me;
Wayne, who taught me patience and self-pride;
Patrick, a pillar and friend forever;
and Anthony Robbins, who taught me to believe in myself,
the human spirit, and passion

ACKNOWLEDGMENTS

There are so many people who have helped me in so many ways that it's almost inevitable that I'll forget to list an important name. Please forgive me if that name is yours.

First and foremost, I have to thank God for giving me the strength to see this project through. This labor of love consumed my life for years, and my resolve was tested heavily, but I was not alone.

To my literary agents, Jan Miller and Dean Williamson—thanks for believing in me. You're awesome!

To my editor, Rick Horgan, whose comments and ideas helped take this work from a pile of reckless pages to something we can all be proud of.

Thanks to my family for their faith and encouragement: Mom and Pop, Dad and Karen, Jim and Patricia.

Thank you, Paul and Marie Jones, my grandparents, for always being there. I love you both very much.

Thanks to my friends at Merrill Lynch—Nick, Ray, Jim, David, and Bobby—for sticking by me when things got tough. Also, thanks to the support staff, Jeanne, Rhonda, and Ann, who kept me on top of things when I was traveling. And to my friend Phil Dodson, for all your effort on my behalf.

Thanks to Curtis Cordova for being so positive and such a good sounding board—you're a dear friend. Thanks to Leslie Becker for her invaluable support and direction throughout the process—I cherish our unlikely and wonderful friendship.

To Joe Vitale, you were the first to believe in me and your instruction proved invaluable. Thank you.

Thanks to Carolyn Rangel at Robbins Research—you're wonderful. And to Anthony Robbins, whose work and generosity has supported me in so many ways: You are a true role model of possibility.

To my loving wife, Cindy, whose faith, inspiration, and tolerance for my odd, long hours has guided me to new levels. You've made this journey, as well as every day of my life, the most joyous experience in the world. Thanks for making me the luckiest and happiest man alive. WTW—I love you!

Thank you all for your faith in my vision.

AUTHOR'S NOTE

The Five Rituals of Wealth was designed for readers at all stages of financial development. A few will have already mastered some of these wealth-building techniques. I applaud them. For those individuals, this book may be used as an opportunity to fine-tune skills and strengthen the knowledge they already possess.

Most readers, though, will be starting at ground zero. If you're among this group, please know that I have great respect for you. Purchasing and reading this book represents a giant leap toward your financial freedom. This book should be retained as a guide through each stage of financial development. You should master each section before going to the next, and refer to the text often when you feel that your skills need improvement.

I should point out that *The Five Rituals of Wealth* would not have been possible without the inspiration of a man named Anthony Robbins. I took his advice years ago, and my life has been forever changed. I strongly suggest familiarizing yourself with the work of Robbins, if you haven't already. He's an eloquent advocate of personal development. His philosophy is this: Judge by results. If something works for you, use it; if not, discard it.

I sincerely hope that this book will work for you. I truly believe that if the five rituals described here are faithfully followed, they will lead toward financial freedom and, in the process, help the spirit to flourish.

FOREWORD

Money—is it a source for contribution, a vehicle for achieving your dreams, or the root of all evil? Do you use it as a weapon or as an instrument of freedom? Does it bring power and security or is it simply a means to an uncertain end?

The largest factor in determining our wealth, or lack of it, is how much of our inherent intelligence and discipline we employ. The depth of potential we access is controlled by our belief systems—our sense of certainty about how difficult or easy it is to earn financial abundance or our beliefs as to what our chances of success are. But equally key is the energy we expend to tackle this area—the amount of emotional complexity we link to learning, or the stamina dedicated to successfully investing our capital and producing financial abundance. Virtually more than anything else, these feelings, emotions, and beliefs determine whether or not we follow through, and are the most significant factors in determining whether or not we will use what we've learned. We must remember that all human behavior is belief driven.

So often in life, people want to change the financial results of their lives, but they fail to address the real cause. Yes, we need a clear plan, which Tod has addressed in his five-step strategy: 1) Pay yourself first, 2) seek your dream, 3) maintain a plan, 4) employ your resources, and 5) act with impact.

But he also focuses on this "invisible force," your core beliefs about money and finance, which are shaping whether you believe you are living a life of abundance or not. His book holds within it the key to unlock whatever has held you back in the past by giving you a methodology to follow that is clear, precise, and simple. He shows you what to do, what could hold you back, and how to make changes that are lasting and effective. The outcome is learning to balance your financial needs with the other important areas of your life: your emotional, physical, contribution, relationship, and time management needs.

Through his thoughtful explanations, Tod passes on to you, the reader, the excitement of being a part of the free enterprise system and a reminder of what truly drives us—our desire to contribute and connect with those around us.

I am proud to have had Tod as a student, to see him graduate to the level of instructor—to be able to call him a friend. I know, through this work, he will positively influence the lives of people around the world!

Life changes only when you act on what you learn. Don't just read Tod's work—take his insight, knowledge, and the strategies he offers and act on them. If you do take action, I am sure his book will be your first step in achieving the level of wealth you desire and deserve. Live with passion!

ANTHONY ROBBINS
DECEMBER 1994

CONTENTS

PASSIVE WEALTH CREATION

PART 4
EVIDENCE OF MASTERY

PART 1

THE
RITUAL
OF
WEALTH

WEALTH:
WHAT WE ALL WANT

Wealth to us is not mere material for vain-glory but an opportunity for achievement, and poverty we think it no disgrace to acknowledge but a real degradation to make no effort to overcome.

—THUCYDIDES, 413 B.C.

ISRAEL 1955: A ten-year-old boy picks up a violin for the first time. It is a seemingly normal occurrence, yet this boy is not normal. In an attempt to overcome the crippling effects of polio, he moves about with braces on both legs, making even the most routine task almost unbearable. His name is Itzhak Perlman. In three years he'll travel to America to battle the disease with the aid of new medical research performed by Jonas Salk. At age nineteen Itzhak will debut at Carnegie Hall and become one of the most respected violinists of his generation. But that unknown future lends little relief on this day as he tediously prepares for his first lesson.

At about the same time, at his home in New York City, an American millionaire named Armand Hammer tunes in to Walter Cronkite's "21st Century" on his black-and-white television set. Jonas Salk is being interviewed about his new Salk Institute and the development of history's first effective polio vaccine. Hammer immediately picks up the phone and makes an appointment to meet the man who could help rid humanity of this crippling disease.

At their meeting, Hammer asks Salk, "Can you possibly tackle cancer the same way you're beating polio?" After all, Hammer thinks, destroying cancer could alter the destiny of the world in unfathomable ways. How many more musicians, artists, and scientists could be freed of this deadly affliction and allowed to make history?

> **Riches are not an end of life, but an instrument of life.**
>
> —HENRY WARD
> BEECHER

"Theoretically," Salk replies. "It ought to be possible to develop a cancer vaccine. But it would cost a tremendous amount of money."

"How much?"

"Five million dollars, for a start."

"All right. I'll give you five million dollars. Go to work," Hammer says without hesitation. Armed with the vision of two men, the Center for Cancer Research at the Salk Institute in California is established.

What is this wealth we all desire? It is the power to think about things that ordinary folks can't even imagine. Things like curing cancer or polio or world hunger. Things like space exploration and quantum physics. The wealthy have a luxury most people don't have. They have the ability to continually express the compassionate, human side of themselves. They have the power to stop being small and selfish and make a difference in the world around them.

In this sense wealth is a condition not only of abundance but of selflessness. It goes beyond money. Being wealthy is being healthy, happy, compassionate, and loving. It is both an application of power and an exercise in humility—a free-flowing tool that we're sometimes allowed to direct but never entirely control.

THE RITUAL OF WEALTH

Most fundamentals of wealth building go back to ancient times. John Jacob Astor said, "Wealth is largely a result of habit." It's absolutely true. I've read countless books on finance, been exposed to the best training in the securities industry, interviewed many wealthy people. And I've found one thing to be absolutely true of those who control vast resources: They don't just do wealthy things once in a while when they feel like it. They habitually live in a state of wealth. They take certain actions over and over again, consistently following routines that allow them to create and maintain considerable wealth. They save, dream, plan, invest, and give—in a never-ending cycle.

They don't just act wealthy every now and then; they *are* wealthy.

Anyone who makes a study of the financial elite recognizes that behind their routines or habits lie consistent core beliefs. In the pages that follow, I've condensed each of these beliefs into one brief statement and linked it to the corresponding habit being discussed.

But before proceeding to that very important constellation of habits and beliefs, let me bring up a belief about money that I think everyone shares to some degree. It goes something like this:

> **The money I have is in direct proportion to the value I've given to others. The more I give of myself, incredibly, the more economic power comes my way. I accept this wealth and prosperity and use its power wisely. Because of this, I can maintain control of some of the wealth that flows through me for the benefit of myself, my family, and my estate.**

If you haven't already done so, make this core belief your own. Believe that you are wealthy. You are! If you live in a highly industrialized country, then regardless of your financial situation, you are wealthier than the majority of the world. For most Americans, food, clothing, and shelter are relatively accessible. Americans can use roads, libraries, museums, and public transportation systems, all at little or no expense. Sometimes it's easy to lose perspective—to forget that 25 percent of the world's population lives on less than $200 a year and that 90 million people live on less than $75 per year.

Wealth, in financial terms, is a measure of value we create for others and a result of the difference we make while alive. It is one measure of the level of our contribution. And yet, tragically, many hardworking, deserving people spend their whole lives contributing only to end up financial failures. In a world where opportunity is unlimited, role models are abundant, and financial counseling is accessible, most people still fail to achieve financial independence. It is in recognition of this state of affairs that my entire professional life has been spent asking such questions as: How is enormous wealth created and maintained by individuals with seemingly no special skills, talents, or contacts, while the majority of the population continues to remain financially dependent? What do the wealthy few do differently on a consistent basis? What habits have they developed that allow them to achieve their dreams? And just as important, what do the financial failures *not* do?

Those are tough questions, but the answers I found are amazingly simple.

In fact, most wealthy people could tell you in five minutes what it takes to experience financial abundance. The problem is, most people don't follow through on the simple habits that can free them almost instantly from financial insecurity. If you do make a commitment, then I promise you, wealth will wrap its arms around you for the rest of your life. If you find that hard to believe, I challenge you to put these timeless suggestions into practice. I've never heard of anyone who lived by these philosophies in some form who didn't achieve financial freedom. It's time to try them for yourself!

DREAM TRAPS

In searching for the reasons why so many people fail drastically to achieve financial independence while others create magnificent wealth and value for others, I uncovered some of the traps people fall into that keep them from reaching their financial goals. These "dream traps" tragically rob millions of people of economic security. And the worst part is that because most of these traps go undetected, undesirable habits are passed on from generation to generation. This book is focused on uncovering these traps and avoiding them by developing new sets of habits and supportive beliefs—rituals, if you will.

As I see it, there are five major dream traps:

1. Failure to make wealth a priority by responsibly managing the resources we already possess
2. Failure to find lifework that expresses our best self and creates total abundance
3. Failure to set goals and plan for our financial future
4. Failure to let the free enterprise system work for us and our money
5. Failure to use money as a tool to create value for ourselves and others

Let us discuss each of these dream traps in detail.

DREAM TRAP 1:
FAILURE TO MAKE WEALTH A PRIORITY BY RESPONSIBLY MANAGING THE RESOURCES WE ALREADY POSSESS

Procrastination is absolutely the greatest barrier to the *passive* accumulation of wealth. Time works for the investor via compound interest. Given enough time, your money grows exponentially like a snowball rolling down a mountain. If you don't begin saving and investing as soon as possible, you lessen the effect dramatically. Let me give you an example.

If I were your fairy godmother, which of these two wishes would you rather I grant you: a million dollars cash right now, or a magic penny that doubles itself every day?

You may have already heard this example in some form before— probably when you were a kid, or from your kids. If you have, reintroduce yourself to it. If you haven't, let me share with you its lesson.

Given the choice, most people would opt for the million dollars. And that wouldn't necessarily be a bad decision. After all, a million dollars is a million dollars! But the far wiser choice is the magic penny that doubles itself every day. Let's look at what would happen to its value over time.

MAGIC DAILY DOUBLING PENNY

Day 2: 2¢
Day 3: 4¢
Day 4: 8¢

Here's where it gets interesting:

Day 28: $1,342,177.00
Day 29: over $2.6 million
Day 38: just over $1 billion—that's *billion* with a *B*
Day 45: well over $1 trillion—that's twelve zeros!

> What folly, to dread the thought of throwing away time at once, and yet have no regard to throwing it away by parcels and piecemeal.
>
> —JOHN HOWE

You get the point. I guess that after a few months of this you'd own the universe. As silly as that example is, I think it has tremendous value. Time is the key to compound interest. The real leverage—the snowball effect—comes in later years when an individual's investment and savings habits have already been formed. Make every effort to develop those good habits now. You certainly won't double your money every day, but the results, factoring in a reasonable rate of return, are almost as staggering.

As a financial consultant, I meet many people who wait until relatively late in life to think about saving as a way to create wealth. They have so far to go in such a little amount of time that it's a major adjustment trying to save enough to retire comfortably on. Early in their lives they had stumbled into that financial-procrastination trap, and now they're paying the price.

So many times we manage our affairs on a crisis basis. Only the things that are extremely urgent get handled immediately. The bills get paid so the lights stay on. We pick up the phone when it rings. We have to run an "important errand"—there's an oxymoron if I've ever heard one. We need that new car—today. There's a huge sale at Saks. The report was due yesterday! Some of these things *are* important, some are just distractions. Unfortunately, in order to get the monkey off our back we jump to take care of trivial urgencies. Time being limited, we sometimes put off the things that don't seem extremely urgent at the time but are so important to living fulfilled and happy lives over the long term.

Think about that for a minute or two. How many times are truly important things—family, personal growth, quality time, financial freedom—put off in favor of things that don't matter much in the long run? *Now* is the time to stop such harmful procrastination. As Goethe, the eighteenth-century writer, once said, "Things which matter most must never be at the mercy of the things which matter least."

I believe most people see financial security as a high priority. It just doesn't seem pressing until we near old age or retirement, and sometimes it's too late. Make a conscious decision now to spend less time and fewer resources on minor "emergencies" and more on seemingly less urgent but high-value

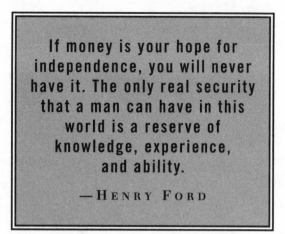

If money is your hope for independence, you will never have it. The only real security that a man can have in this world is a reserve of knowledge, experience, and ability.

—HENRY FORD

priorities. Always remember: Time is on your side as an investor. Don't let it slip through your hands thinking, "Someday I'll get started saving for my future." As the saying goes, *someday* is a road that leads to *nowhere*.

Another big hurdle people must leap in the area of finances is the impression that what's needed is more, more, more. That tendency to "keep up with the Joneses" can be all-consuming. Many people put off getting married, having children, and planning for their future until they're financially "set." But the truth is, things really never settle down—not if you're continually growing. There's never a "perfect" time to take a look at your spending patterns, to begin disciplining yourself.

I'm talking about controlling your outgo or some form of "budgeting," for lack of a better word. I know the horror that word evokes. It suggests struggle and doing without and extreme sacrifice. I used to feel the same way, until I tried it and got results. My idea of budgeting is not a ball and chain but a liberator. I don't want you to do without. Rather, I want you to get control of your expenses so you can have and do all the things you've been putting off.

When advised to budget, most people respond: "But I just don't have enough money." In fact, most of these individuals have a lot more than they think; they just lack control of it. Making more money is not the answer. The sad truth is that if you're out of control, no matter how much money you earn, you can figure out a way to spend it. Doesn't it amaze you how many wealthy and famous people have financial problems? Some even go bankrupt. This is because they haven't mastered this concept of wealth at its most basic level. Bad budgetary habits, when applied to twice as much money, simply create twice as much havoc.

All of us know people who are constantly needing to get out of a jam only to shortly find themselves back in another jam. Have you noticed that their financial problems seem to get bigger and bigger with every spending mistake? This is a bad habit that eventually causes total financial ruin. Sadly, most of these people truly believe it's the problem's fault. If they can get past this shortfall, "just this one time," they'll be okay and back on track. They must be made to understand that throwing money at the problem will not help. Rather than give them a fish, we must teach these people how to fish for themselves.

When you think of wealthy people, what comes to mind? Probably yachts, expensive homes in exotic places, constant leisure and pampering, country clubs, limousines. In general, Mr. Howell from the television show "Gilligan's Island." While this may be true of a few "super rich"—particularly those living off inherited wealth— my research shows that this vision of the wealthy is incorrect.

Here's a more accurate picture of the average self-made millionaire: a middle-aged (or older) person who drives a moderately priced car, sleeves still rolled up from the day's work, is probably married twenty years or more to the same person, who goes to church, most likely owns or runs a business, has kids and/or grandkids, wears black socks with tennis shoes (just kidding), who works ten hours a day and loves it. This set of characteristics is certainly at odds with the stereotype of someone who is rich, but it's absolutely true. These people are the heart and soul of our financial world. They work hard, vote, save, invest, pay taxes, and are active in their local communities. They are ordinary people who have achieved their goals over time. It's important to note that there are over one million of these "ordinary" millionaires (average net worth $3 to $5 million or more) living in America today.

Of course, a million dollars isn't what it used to be. Nowadays the "really rich" category begins at $10 million and the "super rich" at $50 million and above. Maybe being that rich isn't your goal, but one thing is certain: The accumulation of wealth over time takes understanding, discipline, and effort. And the first step in reaching any financial goal is to take control of the resources you already possess so you will be equipped to achieve the financially abundant future you seek.

DREAM TRAP 2:
FAILURE TO FIND LIFEWORK
THAT EXPRESSES OUR BEST SELF
AND CREATES TOTAL ABUNDANCE

In my research I've found that the most wealthy people seem to love their work. Most are entrepreneurs and business owners who'd rather work than do just about anything else—with the exception of spending time with the people they love and care about. I used to think that it was unhealthy to love your work so much. I thought that these people must love money so much they'd do anything for it. But after interviewing many of them, I found the opposite to be true: They spoke of their contribution in their particular field, their employees, and their customers—and seldom, if at all, mentioned the money they'd earned. I found that it wasn't the money they were most proud of; it was the contribution they felt they were making. What really energized them was the possibility of their business or work outliving them, or leaving an estate for their heirs. In short, these winners were driven by something much larger than simply making a living. They believed in their cause and were committed to seeing it through. Rather than money, it was the vision—the dream they held on to—that motivated them to super success.

Robert Fulghum, author of *All I Really Need to Know I Learned in Kindergarten*, puts it this way: "I've always thought . . . that anyone can make money. Making a life worth living, that's the real test." Hugely successful people seem to realize intuitively that the key to success is committing themselves to an inspiring cause that impacts others in a positive way—something that is larger than themselves.

It follows that one of the most common traps people fall into concerns the type of work they do on a daily basis. Most people take a job and keep their nose to the grindstone for most of their lives, never looking up to see whether they're moving closer or farther away from their dreams. I find it hard to believe that, as human beings, our grand purpose in life is to work only so we can pay the bills. I believe that we all have something greater to offer humanity, something special that holds the key to true lifelong wealth and happiness—a destiny. Our individual mission is to find that special talent, or gift, that we possess and commit ourselves to its growth.

I call this special gift—the thing that consumes us in a positive, productive way—a **lifework**. I know that sounds a little philosophical, but the fact remains: Everyone who has ever achieved significant success, wealth, or fame believed in their heart that they were on a vision quest of some sort. People who see themselves as merely working for a living, with a commitment no deeper than just "getting by," seem to always produce mediocre results.

So if you're in a situation where you're working solely for the money, it's probably a good idea to take a look at where you're heading. If you don't feel like what you're doing day-to-day is making a difference to yourself, your customers, your family, or your company, change it. You must find that something that turns you on—the thing that makes you excited about the possibilities for incredible achievement. You must find and pursue with all your soul that thing that makes you stay up late and get up early because you care so much about its success. You must find something worth committing yourself to, worth putting your name on.

Too many people simply fail to go for it. They just want and wish and continue to get up reluctantly every day to go make a living. Consequently, that's what they get: a living—and not much else. These people don't experience the level of fulfillment, joy, and wealth they deserve because they're only asking of the thing that takes so much time and energy that it provide them with a minimum paycheck.

Please understand: I'm not claiming that it's easy to throw off the shackles of one's humdrum existence. Securing your place in this world requires a love, a passion, a commitment to the form of self-expression that is uniquely your own. But when you have it, the world begins to reward you in a big way. Because with that passion, it is possible to reach new heights of productivity—to offer something that no one else can match.

DREAM TRAP 3:
FAILURE TO SET GOALS AND PLAN
FOR OUR FINANCIAL FUTURE

Did you know that most people spend more time planning a two-week vacation than they do their financial future? Many don't think about their financial future at all.

Planning a trip to Disneyland may take five to ten hours or more, whereas a few hours with your broker or financial planner, or just by yourself, could lay the groundwork for lifelong financial success. Yet most people are just "too busy" to do what it takes to be successful in this area. We all know intuitively that saving and planning consistently will get us where we want to go. And most of us know that time and good habits work to our advantage. Then why don't more people succeed in the area of finances? I believe the answer lies in the failure to appreciate just how important goals are.

There's one key aspect to goal setting: If you don't know where you're going, you'll never know when you get there—or if you get there at all. Planning and goal setting are powerful tools. I write down every goal I have in a journal. I also write down the reasons I want to achieve this goal, along with the costs of achieving it. This methodology is powerful because if you can create compelling reasons to achieve your goal, you'll find a way to make it happen. If the costs are too high (too much time, too much money, too risky, etc.), you can abandon the goal and save valuable time and energy. This is one reason that I've achieved every goal I've ever written down. By taking some time to analyze the rewards and costs beforehand, I could make a decision about whether it was worth the time and effort.

You may have heard it said that a goal not written is merely a wish. You shouldn't just wish and hope things will turn out okay. Create a plan and put it into action. Decide what the costs are, and if they're worth it, go for it. Too many people fail to achieve their goals either because they're not committed or because they're not honest about the costs involved. They set goals like: I want a mansion, a Porsche, a jet airplane, world peace, and a perfect family. All of these things are probably achievable, but they involve a huge cost, a huge commitment. Before setting a goal, always make sure that you're willing to pay the price. If you are, you'll be amazed at what you can achieve.

Remember when Steven Spielberg's movie *E.T.* was trampled by *Gandhi* in the Oscar race, and the television show "M*A*S*H" ran its last episode? Remember when quarterback Joe Montana led the San Francisco 49ers to victory over the Cincinnati Bengals in Super Bowl XV? I remember it like it was yesterday. That was

1983! Isn't it amazing how quickly time passes? In the next decade millions—perhaps billions—of people will fail and succeed. Some will retire or die in financial straits and dependency, others will amass tremendous fortunes, live their dreams, and create tremendous value for others in the process. Don't let another day pass without putting your own plan into action. Use this book as a tool; refer to it often. But, most important, use your power to take care of the financial planning you know you need to do. Soon you'll begin to enjoy the financial success you deserve.

DREAM TRAP 4:
FAILURE TO LET THE FREE ENTERPRISE SYSTEM WORK FOR US AND OUR MONEY

In today's world, millionaires are created every day and new technology is developed at lightning speed. Millions of dollars are made and lost on world stock exchanges, sometimes before 10:00 A.M.! In this global society you don't have to be an inventor or financial wizard to achieve financial success. In some cases all you have to do is piggyback onto those who have talent for wealth creation. The best vehicle I know of for making your money work as hard as you do is the stock market—accessed through mutual funds.

I realize that the thought of participating in the stock market sends chills through many people, but I don't mean gambling in the market. I'm talking about simply taking advantage of the magnificent free enterprise system, which allows you to invest via the stock market in companies, their talented management, and their technology, as well as participate in their profits.

If you drove by a billboard a few years ago that was advertising cellular phones and said, "Wow, I know those are going to be in every car or briefcase in America," yet failed to invest in the industry, you should be shot! (Just kidding.) If you went into America's number 1 department store, Wal-Mart, ten years ago and thought it was a great store but didn't become a part owner of the company via a stock purchase, you should be hanged! (Please don't do it—for illustrative purposes only.) If there is a new development, product, or service—or even an old one—that is in demand, chances are you can participate in its success through a public company. You can own a part of the company without ever lifting a finger to create and market the product yourself. That is nothing less than amazing.

It may sound hyperbolic to say so, but I believe it to be true: *Never before in the history of the world have so many people had the opportunity to be wealthy beyond their wildest dreams.* Investing for the long term can be almost as simple as picking up the phone and investing in a stock mutual fund. And if you don't know what to do, there is professional help. You can hire the best money managers in the world for pennies on the dollar. It's cheap!

Why do so many people fail to let the system work for them to help create financial abundance? I believe the answer is pure and simple: ignorance. Many people fail to devote any time to understanding the financial markets. The rudiments of how the markets work are rarely taught in schools. For many people, this lack of financial know-how kills hopes and dreams for a better life. It's because I'm so acutely aware of the gap in the average person's knowledge about how to profit from the free enterprise system that I've written this book.

DREAM TRAP 5: FAILURE TO USE MONEY AS A TOOL TO CREATE VALUE FOR OURSELVES AND OTHERS

Yes, I'm talking about giving. I believe that the failure to give is probably the most common mistake people make on their road to riches. When we're out there in the dog-eat-dog world just trying to get our share, we sometimes forget to enjoy our wealth and prosperity. We forget to give something back. Sometimes we even hoard. We want what we *think* money will give us—the value, the power, the opportunity, the freedom, the security, and the fun it creates. Yet we can't take it with us, and hoarding does no good for anyone.

When you experience success financially, it's imperative that you contribute to a worthwhile cause. This accomplishes several things. First, there's the joy of being able to make a difference. Knowing that you left this world a little better is an unbelievable feeling. Second, the act of giving enables you to relax, to realize that there is enough to go around. You see that your needs are really met and that you have abundance. Third, while it's true that the left hand should never know what the right hand is doing, there's no question that giving encourages others to act in a reciprocal fashion—sometimes out of all proportion to the original gesture.

I think each of us should try to give away at least 10 percent of our income. I know how difficult it is to manage, but it can yield immeasurable results. While there's nothing magic about that 10 percent number, it *is* both generous and practical—hence, the reason it's long been suggested as a standard charitable contribution.

Becoming a giver and using your abilities to help other people often comes back to an individual tenfold. I've seen many instances of this principle at work. I'm sure you have too. People tend to believe this law of wealth. Of course, actually writing the check is a different story. Most people put off giving, thinking that when they become "rich" they'll instantly become a pillar of the community and do good things. But remember: The habits you develop now will most likely stay with you a lifetime. How likely is it, really, that your habit of declining to give will change once your wallet is stuffed with money?

I can't offer exact numerical data on the returns you'll see if you make charitable contribution a part of your life, but I will offer you this:

Most people would consider J. P. Morgan, the banker, financier, and philanthropist who flourished around the turn of the century, one of the wealthiest men in American history. During a visit to an Ivy League medical school he was asked to consider partially funding new medical-research buildings. He was in a hurry and told the staff to quickly show him the plans. The plans were barely spread out when Morgan pointed to three buildings and said, "I'll give that, and that, and that," and rushed from the room before he could even be thanked.

That's power! That's what wealth is all about: the ability to make a difference—maybe even a priceless contribution to mankind—by pointing a finger. And if you think that J. P. Morgan's generosity began after he became wealthy, you're mistaken and missing the point. The fact is: The chance to impact the world in a tremendous way was what drove Morgan to create magnificent wealth.

If you don't remember anything else I say on the subject of charitable contribution, remember this illustrative question: *Is it easier to give away one-tenth of a day's pay or one-tenth of an estate?* In other words, is it easier to give away $10 out of $100 or $100,000 out of your first million?

The point I keep coming back to is that giving is a habit just like anything else. Believe me, no matter how fortunate you are, a hundred thousand dollars is still a hundred thousand dollars. If you can't become a giver on a smaller salary, you'll be unlikely to give when your income becomes much larger. That insight has forced me to take a look at my own contribution habits. I hope it helps you as well.

One final note on giving. I can't claim that giving is a prerequisite to amassing a pile of money, because there are so many obviously greedy people getting rich. However, I never consider these people wealthy, and I've seen a lot of them fall hard in the last few years. As I've said before, wealth goes beyond money. It means abundance and prosperity, but it also means health, happiness, loving, caring, sharing, learning. It is the opportunity to make a difference.

The Bible says it best: "What is a man profited, if he shall gain the whole world, and lose his own soul?" Don't work your fingers to the bone hoarding your first million and lose sight of who you really are: an abundant, compassionate giver!

FUNDAMENTAL RECIPE FOR MASTERING THE FIVE RITUALS OF WEALTH

INGREDIENTS:
- Commitment to wealth
- Faith in the free enterprise system
- Patient understanding of the relationship between time and money

COMMITMENT TO WEALTH

Having a fire in the belly for the creation and accumulation of wealth is paramount. A strong desire can overcome many mistakes and shortfalls. What is this commitment I'm talking about? It's a belief that you can win! It's making having wealth a priority, not just a wish. It's a belief that you have all the brains, talent, and drive necessary to create your own personal fortune.

Most people would like to have money, but are they *committed* to having it? We know the statistics—the large majority of our population is relatively penniless, and that's sad. Is commitment something we can create? I think so. There are amazing new methods in the area of human development that can speed you to your goal. Certainly, it's worth trying to develop that kind of mind-set, because Calvin Coolidge's famous quote remains as true today as when he uttered it decades ago:

Nothing in the world can take the place of persistence!

Talent will not—nothing is more common than unsuccessful men with talent!

Education will not—the world is full of educated derelicts!

Genius will not—unrewarded genius is almost a proverb!

Persistence and determination alone are omnipotent!

Having a commitment to wealth means becoming a student of wealth. You should read about money, finance, investment, and taxes; meet people who are wealthy and learn from them; make wealth education your focus—your hobby. Don't mistake me. I don't want you to become an Ebenezer Scrooge and neglect everything in life for the sake of money. Have balance, yes, but also be a lifelong learner in the area of wealth. If you want anything in life—a good family, a rewarding career, fame—you've got to work at it. Why should creating an estate that will support you and your family be any different? Look over the Suggested Reading list at the back of this book. Pick out a few titles and begin there.

Also, learn from the results you experience—not just from other people's opinions. Take what you can use and discard what doesn't work. There are no absolutes. I see too many people following one source, one opinion. That single opinion may have merit, but become informed enough to draw from many experts and form your own conclusions. It's your life and your money!

One area that must be mastered is taxes. Tax laws change every few years, sometimes radically, and you must be continually up to speed. Roughly one-third of all the income you'll make in your lifetime will go the government. You need to be informed so you can pay the appropriate tax—and not a penny more! If you feel like being patriotic, put those extra resources to work locally—toward a cause where you can see a direct impact.

One way to strengthen your commitment to wealth is to form alliances with people who have a sincere interest in helping you achieve your dreams. Believe me, there are plenty of these people out there—true professionals who take an interest in their clients' well-being. Get to know a stockbroker or financial planner, an accountant, an insurance agent, a tax attorney, and an estate-planning specialist. Some professionals claim to be all of these, and some are, but I think it's important to have a group of support people who represent a range of different opinions.

You may be tempted to go it alone. That's okay, but I've found that, even with my experience in the financial field, monitoring the changes in our economic, legal, and legislative environments is a monumental task. Accordingly, I rely on experts constantly. Good attorneys, brokers, or accountants will pay for themselves many times over.

FAITH IN THE FREE ENTERPRISE SYSTEM

Today highly industrialized countries face a multitude of socio-economic and environmental problems. For that reason, it's sometimes tempting to fantasize about moving to a remote tropical island where people barter for what they want and there's no such thing as taxes. But reality reminds us of an unassailable fact: From an investment perspective, the free enterprise system works! Anyone who's ever placed his faith in it has always been right.

The easiest way to participate in the growth of a country's economic base is through the stock market—passively owning a part of the corporations that make and sell widgets. I know, it sounds risky. But, as I've said before, I'm not talking about gambling or trading in the market. I'm talking about sound, long-term investing. Some might ask, "If the system is so good, why doesn't everyone participate?" The answer is: emotion. The twin emotions of fear and greed cause volatility in the markets.

Why do people fear the market? Well, for one thing, stock prices go up and down on a daily basis. Investors tend to forget that quality issues eventually recover their value, and advance higher, given enough time. Also, the media plays a large role in instilling fear in potential investors. In current financial reporting there's a misleading emphasis on who the biggest stock market winners and losers are on a given day. Journalists treat it as a big deal if IBM goes up a point or McDonald's goes down two. Never mind that a few points are usually insignificant; besides, it's history! You'll never see a journalist declare: "Another normal day on Wall Street as average investors continued to hold their positions and create long-term wealth by participating in the growth of our economic base." The report would be the same every day, and there'd be no need for financial journalists!

I can't tell you how many calls I get from investors wanting to buy the biggest-winning stock of the day. That's greed. Why someone would want to buy a stock after it's made headlines with a huge run, I'll never know. I also hear concerns about stocks that lose a few points. That's fear. While some news developments give us insight into the future earnings of the company, the vast majority of these "significant events" are not especially meaningful.

It's true that the American stock market has experienced some tough times—we've had twenty-six bear (down) markets in the last hundred years. We've had more bull (up) markets in that time period, but the fact remains that stocks do go down too. If this bothers you, ask yourself two questions:

- Is it true that in the last two hundred years every single time the American stock market has fallen (some use the terms *declined*, *slumped*, *corrected*, or worse—*crashed*) it has always come back?
- Is it true that every single time the market has come back it has eventually gone on to set new highs?

The answer to both of these questions is yes!

The most critical element of successful investing is time—not timing. If you do decide to own stocks, either independently or through a stock mutual fund, don't make the mistake of trying to predict financially significant events. Just know that you're going to go through some uncertain times, and stay invested. It sounds smart to avoid down markets, but the fact is, no one can look into a crystal ball and accurately predict the stock market. Trying to avoid down markets will only cause you to miss out on up markets.

As with anything in life, you can't focus on burying what you've got: You must focus on creating, saving, and investing—trying to grow. That means choosing a sound investment program and, unless something radical occurs, sticking to your guns. Have faith in the free enterprise system.

PATIENT UNDERSTANDING OF THE RELATIONSHIP BETWEEN TIME AND MONEY

In investing, the most common variables people overlook are the all-important relationships between time, money, rates of return, and inflation. These relationships are important because it is impossible to plan without making some assumptions about each. For example, suppose you'd saved $100,000 (a substantial sum of money) and decided to retire with it today. Let's say you took all the interest from your $100,000 in the form of an income stream over the next twenty-five years and spent it. Your idea was to keep your principal ($100,000) intact. You succeeded. Now it's twenty-five years later and you still have your money. What's the value of your hard-earned savings? You say, "One hundred thousand dollars, of course." That's true, but what if I told you that a new car will cost you $105,000, your food bill is $1,500 a month, and your electric bill is now $6,000 a year? Now what is your $100,000 worth? There's an important lesson here: *Money value is not important. Purchasing power is all that matters.*

We've all heard stories of our parents or grandparents working for "a dollar a day" in the "good old days" and living just fine. Inflation exists today and probably will forever. It is the investor's worst enemy. I'll discuss how to battle inflation later, but for now, understand that merely setting a monetary goal is not enough, you must consider how to overcome the factors that have a direct impact on standard of living.

Inflation is the bad news. The good news is the relationship between time and money: the time value of money. As an investor, this is by far the greatest factor working in your favor. If you have time, you don't need to save a lot of money to reach your goal. Unfortunately, the reverse is also true: the less time you have, the more you'll need to save. For example, if your goal is to become a millionaire by retirement and you have forty years to achieve it (perhaps you're a twenty-five-year-old who wants to retire at sixty-five), you'll need to save only $85 a month for the next forty years to reach that million-dollar mark (assuming a 12 percent yield).

If you have the same goal of millionaire status and you're forty-five aiming for retirement at age sixty-five, you'll need to put away ten times that amount in the next twenty years: about $1,011 a month! What a difference time and compound interest can make. Along those same lines, if you can achieve a 15 percent return for the next twenty years (as opposed to the 12 percent return assumed in the earlier examples), you'll need to sock away only about $668 a month. Don't underestimate the effect of rate of return—especially over the long term.

The "fundamental recipe" above is a summary of the foundational beliefs necessary for mastering the rituals of wealth and using them in a way that creates incredible riches. However, the secret to harnessing their power lies in understanding the difference between elements that are out of your control (e.g., the market, the economy, interest rates) and the elements that are in your control, namely, consistent and constructive financial habits—what I call "rituals of wealth." These rituals are the only factors over which you have direct and complete jurisdiction. Without them, all the financial planning and business opportunities in the world are useless.

You must develop habits that cause you to continually *act*! You can uncover a multimillion-dollar idea, the stock market can have its greatest run in history, and the economy can grow at unprecedented rates, and it will be meaningless to your financial future unless you're in there claiming your share.

I'll shortly be talking about each of the five wealth rituals in depth, but for now, let me just list them. Each ritual consists of a two part phrase: the *habit* and its underlying *belief.* Write them down and

REACHING MILLIONAIRE STATUS

Monthly Savings Amount Needed at Various Rates of Return

Time to Retirement	4%	8%	12%	15%
10 Years (120 months)	$6,793	$5,469	$4,347	$3,634
15 Years (180 months)	4,065	2,892	2,002	1,496
20 Years (240 months)	2,728	1,699	1,011	668
25 Years (300 months)	1,946	1,053	532	308
30 Years (360 months)	1,441	672	286	144
35 Years (420 months)	1,095	437	156	68
40 Years (480 months)	847	287	85	32

memorize them if you have to. I list them in my day planner and review them daily. Do whatever works for you—just make sure they become as much a part of your regular routine as brushing your teeth, and you'll grow wealthier than you ever imagined.

The five rituals of wealth are:
1. Pay yourself first; it's okay to keep some.
2. Seek your dream; if you do what you love, the money will follow.
3. Maintain a plan; the map becomes the territory.
4. Employ your resources; money goes where it's treated best.
5. Act with impact; you've got to give to live.

I know they sound simple. They are! The reason these lessons are as old as money itself and have remained relatively unchanged is this: They work! The difficulty lies not in understanding them but in practicing them. Most people can agree on the way to accumulate wealth; unfortunately, only a few have the vision and discipline to make it happen.

HOW TO USE THIS BOOK EFFECTIVELY

For the purpose of this book, I've adapted *Webster's* definition of *ritual* as follows:

> *ritual*: **any consistent <u>action</u>, taken with congruent <u>belief</u>, that supports advancement in the direction of a desirable end result**

In other words, a ritual is an action taken for a cause that you strongly believe in! It's the marriage of a habit and an underlying belief.

Habits that don't support us in our beliefs have no value. In fact, such habits are usually destructive and are the ones we're always trying to change. For example: If you believe smoking is bad for you, and you smoke, that's a habit you know you must eventually change. On the other hand, if you believe smoking is bad for you, and you never smoke, that's a habit that should be supported. My point is: Positive habits are born out of some specific belief.

Since beliefs are the building blocks of greatness, it's important we define *belief* as well:

> *belief*: **an absolute conviction that something is true or valid**

Beliefs are learned. They are the residue of education and experience. They help us make decisions. We know that we shouldn't jump off a building, because jumping from great heights in the past has caused us pain. We realize, without question, that it's an action that shouldn't be taken. Most of our beliefs serve us well. Some, though, do not. Some are actually destructive.

Unfortunately, many beliefs aren't obtained from the most qualified sources. Learning about diet from parents who have unhealthy eating habits isn't recommended. Nor is accepting enthusiastic views on smoking from the profiting tobacco company's advertisements.

The same applies in the area of personal finance. Unfortunately, most of us are taught about wealth and money by people who have good intentions but lack exper-tise. Worse, some pass on advice that is downright awful. I've actually had people tell me, for exam-ple, that money is the root

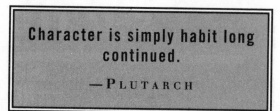

Character is simply habit long continued.

—PLUTARCH

of all evil. As it happens, I share George Bernard Shaw's opposing and, in this case, supportive belief: *Lack of money is the root of all evil.* It's always seemed to me that people's dark sides get exposed when they lack resources. Also, those who complain that the wealthy are evil and mean have created no wealth themselves, anyway. So why use them as financial role models?

One of the goals of this book is to help you form positive, supportive beliefs about money.

The key to strengthening supportive beliefs is continually feeding yourself supportive references or cues. At the same time you should be disempowering the references that hinder you—by questioning their validity and removing them from the fabric of your life.

This book aims to reinforces these supportive beliefs with compelling, factual arguments and to disarm false and destructive beliefs about wealth and money. The goal is to give you the tools necessary to create tremendous wealth.

By stating each of the five key rituals as a linked two-part phrase—the first part being the *habit* and the second the underlying *belief*—this book provides an airtight method for mentally mastering its principles. For example:

Wealth Ritual 1: Pay yourself first; it's okay to keep some.

"Pay yourself first" is the habit that must be developed to succeed financially and avoid Dream Trap 1: failure to make the accumulation of wealth a priority.

"It's okay to keep some" is the underlying belief that encourages the development of this habit of saving by paying yourself first. Once you change your core belief, the habit falls into line and becomes a part of your identity, pulling you toward your dreams. The failure to believe that it's okay to keep some is the cause of most people's inability to pay themselves first. No matter how hard they

> We sow our thoughts,
> and we reap our actions.
> We sow our actions,
> and we reap our habits.
> We sow our habits,
> and we reap our character.
> We sow our character,
> and we reap our destiny!
>
> —ANONYMOUS

try to save, they can't maintain the self-discipline because they have conflicting beliefs about money. They're asking their body to go against their core beliefs and are frustrated by attempts to change the habit first. So work on changing the belief first by expanding education and experience and acknowledging supportive references and cues. Develop corresponding habits. Then watch those dream traps disappear from your life.

Remember, mastering the five rituals means acquiring five beliefs, developing five habits, and vanquishing five dream traps. It's really pretty simple. I hope you'll agree.

HABIT

I am your constant companion.
I am your greatest helper or heaviest burden.

I will push you onward or drag you down to failure.
I am completely at your command.

Half the things you do you might just as well
turn over to me and I will be able to do them
quickly and correctly.

I am easily managed—
you must merely be firm with me.
Show me exactly how you want
something done and after a few lessons
I will do it automatically.
I am the servant of all great men;
and alas, of all failures, as well.
Those who are great, I have made great.
Those who are failures, I have made failures.

I am not a machine,
though I work with all the precision
of a machine plus the intelligence of a man.
You may run me for a profit or run me for ruin—
it makes no difference to me.

Take me, train me, be firm with me,
and I will place the world at your feet.
Be easy with me and I will destroy you.

Who am I? I am habit!

—ANONYMOUS

WEALTH RITUAL 1

Pay Yourself First—It's Okay to Keep Some

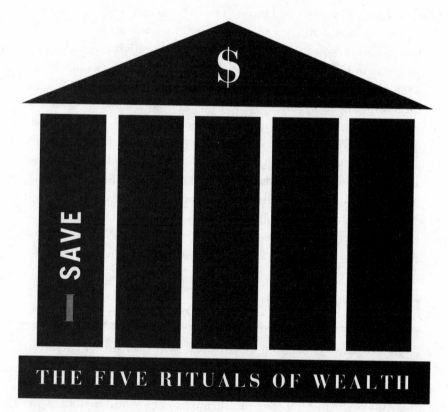

> **The greatest of evils and the worst of crimes is poverty...our first duty—a duty to which every other consideration should be sacrificed—is not to be poor.**
>
> —GEORGE BERNARD SHAW

ON A SUNNY AFTERNOON IN 400 B.C. the Greek philosopher Socrates and a friend leisurely stroll through the Athens marketplace. Socrates stops every now and then to compliment a merchant on his wares, then moves on to the next stand. His friend, noticing the philosopher's interest in the merchandise, asks him why he loves to frequent the market but never purchases anything. "I'm always amazed to see just how many things there are that I don't need," replies Socrates.

So many times we manage our monthly income in a way that prevents us from appreciating the true level of wealth we already have. We pay the butcher, baker, and candlestick maker, and anyone else who cares to sell us something while we're in the mood. We commit our total monthly income and then some—and never really keep any for ourselves. The problem is that we forget to make ourselves just as important as the people who are competing for our hard-earned dollars. *We've given all our economic power away!*

THE WEALTHY MIND-SET

There is a way to become wealthy without ever increasing your income, and it's a lot easier than you think. We're going to discuss why you really don't need any more to live a happy and prosperous life. And we'll find out that by learning to enjoy and manage what you already have, getting more is easier and more fun than ever before. Once you learn to hold on to some of your economic power, in the form of saving, your focus shifts. You stop worrying about every nickel and begin to find enjoyable ways to create substantial wealth. In the last few sections of this book, you'll learn how to finally earn

ker at a large Wall Street brokerage firm, I sat down to make a few dozen cold calls. Most brokers cold-call in the beginning to build a client base. I telephoned a man I'll call Fred Johnson. The call went like this:

"Mr. Johnson, this is Tod Barnhart. I'm a stockbroker at XYZ."

"Whaddya want?" boomed his voice.

"Well, sir, I'd like to help you manage your money wisely," I said confidently.

"I don't have any money!" he replied.

Now, everyone makes mistakes, but in the next few seconds I made a big one—one that changed the direction of my life. Being young and, shall we say, overly confident, I felt Mr. Johnson was putting me on. I actually imagined him as a whale—a huge investor—whose captured business would bring me prestige in the firm. I was also convinced that I was capable of making him another fortune with my market prowess if only he'd send me a few million dollars. I'm embarrassed at my response, but out it came:

"Oh, I know I could shake you upside down and ten grand would fall out of your pockets."

I figured he probably got calls from a hundred brokers a day, that he just wanted to get rid of me, and that my quick-witted response would get his attention.

He said, and I'll never forget his voice: "Son, I retired eight years ago, mandatory. I don't have a dime, and Social Security doesn't cut it. I can't even take care of myself, and I may lose my home. All I have left is regret. If you would have called me twenty years ago—maybe I wouldn't have put off saving for my future. But now it's just too late. Thanks anyway."

I was speechless! I thought almost everybody over the age of fifty or sixty was rich, because they'd had the chance to earn and save for so many years. I just said, "I'm sorry" and hung up, thinking as I did about the pain that had come through that phone. It had to feel horrible to be in such dire financial straits after you'd lived and worked hard most of your life. That short phone call encouraged me to try to help people, including myself, from ever having to be in that position.

I hear this all the time: "But it's so hard." Well, it's easier than you think, and it's certainly easier than becoming a financial statistic. Being a financial failure is what's really hard.

Here's the problem: *Most of us have been taught little or nothing about wealth.* Most people grow up believing they should pay all their bills first and then play with what's left. There's some sense to that strategy. Certainly, it teaches us responsibility as debtors. The thing is, we've never been told that we count as much as our creditors. No one has ever said it's okay to save and pay ourselves first.

The result? By the end of the month we've successfully paid the person that owns our house (mortgage or rent), the person that owns our car, the dry cleaner, the grocer, et cetera. We've paid everyone except ourselves! If you just live by the one rule that *you* count at least as much as your barber when it comes to paying the bills, you can change your life for the better. Immediately, the focus changes from paying bills to investing savings, and you're on your way.

The first ritual of wealth and the most important rule of financial success is: **Pay yourself first; it's okay to keep some.**

The way I see it, there are three basic steps to making any financial change:

1. Realizing that where you are now is *not* exactly where you'd like to be
2. Creating compelling reasons to make a change
3. Putting a well-thought-out plan into action and sticking to it.

The first step, as I've just said, is being aware. Sometimes awareness alone can help people change their finances, but most of us need a little encouragement. People tend to make changes either because they're inspired to experience something, or because there's something they desperately want to avoid.

Of those two motivations, the latter is usually the strongest. Let me give you an example: Which of the following possibilities would cause you to take immediate action to change your finances: the chance to own a dream home on a lake or in the mountains, or the chance you might get thrown out of your apartment because you can't pay the rent?

Now, I've always believed that people will do their best when presented with great opportunity, but what I've seen more often is the flip side: They'll do almost anything to avoid losing what they've got. In a

battle between despera-
tion and inspiration, desperation usually flexes the
most muscle. To para-
phrase Anthony Robbins:
We are controlled by the
twin forces of pain and
pleasure, and most people

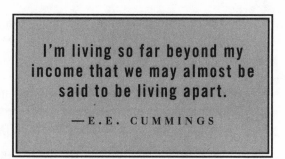

I'm living so far beyond my income that we may almost be said to be living apart.

—E.E. CUMMINGS

will do more to avoid pain than they will ever do to gain pleasure.

In other words, people tend to display more action and fight when they get put into a corner.

What does this have to do with increasing wealth? Well, that takes us to the second step in changing our financial environment: constructive pressure. *If you want to change your financial mind-set, you have to believe in your gut that not having financial security will be more painful than the effort, discipline, and planning required to obtain it.* Just looking at people like the aforementioned Fred Johnson should strengthen your resolve.

Which is not to discount the power of dreams and fantasies. They'll be a help, too—a big help. But when you're faced with that difficult choice of spending money on something you really don't need, I've found that it's easier to derive motivation from the stick than from the carrot. The stakes are high. If you don't hold back at least a bit of your income on a regular basis in the form of savings, you'll eventually find yourself, at retirement time, without options.

The third step in changing your financial situation is the simplest to explain but the most difficult to put into practice. You *must* develop a sound plan to reach your goals, and follow it religiously. We'll spend a great deal of time in later chapters discussing financial plans and how to put yours into effect immediately. For now, decide that you'll make this a priority. You'll begin to make steady progress in the direction of your dreams.

The simple exercise that follows is designed to stir you up a bit. I want to create a little bit of discomfort so you'll see the need to begin paying yourself first immediately. Some people can change their budgeting and savings habits instantly with this exercise. Others need to put more pressure on themselves. That's all right, but make the commitment right now to do whatever it takes to begin changing your thinking and, consequently, your behavior. Give this short exercise your honest effort. It could yield immeasurable results.

FILL IN THE BLANKS PROVIDED BELOW:

Total income you've earned in your lifetime so far
  (salary multiplied by years worked):

_____

Total liquid net worth to date (savings, stocks, bonds, cash,
  etc.):

_____

If you're like most people, you're probably shocked at how much money has passed through your hands in such a short period of time. Measured against your lifetime income, the amount of savings you've accumulated probably seems paltry. The lesson is clear: If you do nothing but change the way you manage the money you already have, it could change your life. If you do nothing but make consistently paying yourself first (in the form of some type of savings/investment plan) a priority, you'll never have to increase your income to become wealthy over time. I have yet to meet anyone who couldn't benefit from improving his skills in this area. *Again, it's not what you earn that makes you wealthy, it's what you keep!*

There's an expression one hears often in reference to getting in shape that I think has application in the financial arena: "Use it or lose it." If you don't consistently use the ability you have to manage your finances properly, eventually that responsibility will be taken away.

The Bible, in Matthew 25:14–29, makes that point abundantly clear:

> **A man, before his journey to another country, called three of his servants together and loaned them money to invest for him while he was gone. He gave ten talents [currency unit] to his servants to manage while he was away. He gave five talents to one servant, two talents to another,**

and one talent to the last—dividing it in proportion to their abilities. He then left for his trip. After a period of time, the master returned from his journey and called upon the servants to account for his money.

The first servant entered with ten talents. He'd invested wisely and could return five more than had been entrusted to him.

"Good work," his master said. "You are a good and faithful servant. You have been faithful over this small amount, so now I will give you much more."

The second servant entered with four talents. He'd invested wisely and could return two more than had been entrusted to him.

"Good work," his master said. "You are a good and faithful servant. You have been faithful over this small amount, so now I will give you much more."

The third servant entered with the one talent he'd been given, and said, "Sir, I knew you were a hard man to please, and I was afraid to lose the only talent you gave me so I buried it and can now return it to you."

The master replied, "You are a wicked and slothful servant! You should have at least made a simple investment so I could have some interest! Take the money from this man and give it to the man with the ten talents. For the man who uses well what he is given shall be given more, and he shall have abundance. But from the man who is unfaithful, even what little responsibility he has shall be taken from him."

All the time I hear people say, "If I just earned more money, then I could feel wealthy or pay my bills or use money as a tool to do good things, or save for my future." The lists seem to go on forever, but believe me when I say: *Before significant wealth will come your way and stay, you have to master the money you already control.*

We all hear about wealthy athletes and entertainers who squander their fortunes because, while they've learned how to earn a lot of money, they don't have the good business sense to master the few universal laws of wealth. A few years ago a newspaper reported that Elvis Presley died with a net worth of $5 million. Now, I don't know how many millions Elvis earned in his career, but for a man who once spent $38,000 on Christmas presents, $5 million in net worth seems like next to nothing. You can probably think of a dozen high-paid, famous people who have been forced into similar financial circumstances by their bad savings habits. All of us find it difficult to save, but it's more difficult at a higher income if good habits haven't already been formed. The habits are still there, and the expenses and problems have gotten a whole lot bigger.

Donald Trump tells a humorous story that really puts things in perspective. At one point he was worth billions and owned a colossal amount of real estate, primarily in New York City. As he tells it, he was walking down the street after he'd been put on a budget by some of the banking institutions to which he owed millions, when he came across a homeless person digging through the trash. This person was obviously worth nothing financially, and Trump's initial reaction was to look down on him. But after a moment's thought, he said, "This man is my superior in financial terms." Someone asked, "How can that be, he's worth nothing." Trump responded, "He's worth nothing, but I'm worth *negative* several hundred million."

That's another world, but you get the idea. We must use what resources we have to the best of our ability, no matter how small or large they may seem at present, if we're ever to hope for more money or financial abundance.

Ben Franklin wrote in *The Way to Wealth* in 1758: "If you would be wealthy, think of saving, as well as of getting. The Indies have not made Spain rich, because her outgoes are greater than her incomes."

I'm not suggesting that you be irresponsible with your debts, merely that you make paying yourself a priority. For your future's sake, you must consistently keep some of what you earn.

I'll show you how to find the money to save shortly, but right now make a decision that you'll begin to develop a new belief that you'll save for yourself first. Make the slogan "It's okay to keep some" your own. Write it in your planner or diary, say it to yourself constantly, and develop that thought pattern.

Keep in mind: *The successful person never becomes bored with fundamentals.* He practices them over and over until his skills are perfected, and then he practices them some more. This is what we call mastery. Wealthy people practice these strategies daily and never get bored.

THE 10 PERCENT SOLUTION

When it comes to saving and investing for your future, the historical rule of thumb is 10 percent. Save 10 percent of your income every single month, and you'll grow wealthier than you dreamed possible. It's sometimes necessary to save more, of course—particularly if you have ambitious retirement dreams. It depends on your age, how long you have until retirement, and the rate of return you earn on your money. *But begin by adopting the belief that 10 percent of everything you earn is yours to keep.*

If you save 10 percent of all you earn for the next ten years, how much money will you have? A year's salary, right? Well, not exactly. You'd also have the interest accumulated on the investments you made over the ten-year period. And that cumulative factor is what makes a "mere" 10 percent a powerful amount to set aside. If you don't save now and can't begin to see where you can get the money, pay special attention to the next section, which discusses budgeting and how to find the money to invest.

One way to save consistently is to get yourself on a monthly or weekly investment plan. Brokerage firms have superb resources in this area—some will even draft your checking account or send you a confirmation when your investment is due. This is called a systematic or automatic investment plan, and it works well with individual retirement accounts (IRAs). Also, your employer may offer some type of tax-deferred savings plan. This is by far the easiest and best way to save because the company will deduct the portion you want saved right out of your check, before you even see it.

CONTROL THE OUTGO

I've said repeatedly in this book that to get more of anything in life, including money, you have to first learn to master what's already been given you. This principle is demonstrated in one of my favorite stories:

> **If it isn't the sheriff, it's the finance company; I've got more attachments on me than a vacuum cleaner.**
>
> —JOHN BARRYMORE

John D. Rockefeller, Jr., one of the wealthiest men in America, once made a collect call from a pay phone that failed to return the money he had put in. He called up the operator, who asked for his name and address so that the money could be mailed to him. Rockefeller began: "My name is John D.—Oh, forget it, you wouldn't believe me anyway."

This is a man who financed the Rockefeller Center in New York City and established many charitable foundations. He'd inherited billions from his father, John D., Sr., but he still knew the value of a dollar. If someone who is this fortunate habitually controls his outgo by watching his expenses that closely, maybe there's a lesson to be learned. And think about this: *As you develop the skills and habits of wealth, you can pass them on to your children and grandchildren, helping to secure their financial future as well.*

The Rockefellers have remained a prosperous family for the last one hundred years because they make it a priority to teach the lessons of wealth and responsibility to their kids. As a third-generation Rockefeller, John D. III knew this principle very well. He wouldn't just give his children their allowances, he would sit down with them and teach them how to direct the money properly. His daughter Alida recalls, "My father would sit down with me, and I got fifteen cents to spend, fifteen cents to save, and fifteen cents to give away. . . . It was our *ritual*." There are enough financial lessons in that example to fill a book in itself, but for the sake of focus let's tackle one in particular.

I'm about to discuss the *B* word. Prepare yourself! Yes, I'm talking about *budgeting*. If you're thinking of skipping these few pages, don't do it! This is an important step in your financial development and fundamental to paying yourself first. The good news is that controlling your expenses is much easier than you think, and once you learn to do it, you'll find money you didn't realize you had. This section is designed to allow you to have *more* of the things you want, not deprive you of the things you love in life.

If you're like most people, awareness alone of where your money goes will give you back control of your finances. If you're not convinced that a budget is necessary, think of how often you go to the cash machine and come away with a stack of twenty-dollar bills only to have it disappear without a trace. Where did it go? What do you have to show for it?

This used to happen to me all the time. I thought I knew where the money was going, but the truth is I didn't. At times my wife and I found ourselves being deprived of the things we truly wanted and deserved because we'd spent a small fortune on things we couldn't trace and probably didn't really want.

Let me give you another scenario: How many times have you planned to pay off your credit cards but only been able to make the minimum payment? You're a responsible person; you don't buy things you can't afford. Why are you going backward?

The easiest and most effective way to make sure you always find the money to pay yourself first is to control the outgo. There *is* a simple way to do this:

Write it down.

Write down in a notebook everything you buy and every dollar you spend, and you'll gain an enormous amount of control over your finances. I know; it worked for me! What immediately happens is that you talk yourself out of making certain purchases because you anticipate the guilt you'll feel when you write them down. You know you'll find yourself saying, how could I have spent money on something so silly? That type of self-awareness is great, because it saves us from the type of impulse purchases that burn holes in our pockets.

Something funny happens when you write down expenditures. They have a way of staring you back in the face and forcing you to make decisions about their value. You'll be asking yourself: "Is this purchase going to keep me from having something else that I truly want?" or, "What's the lost opportunity if I choose to spend my money in this way?" In economics that's called "opportunity cost."

There's a rule of life relating to having things that cost money: *We can truly have anything we desire, if we work for it, but we can't have everything!* Now, you may say, "Tod, I thought you were an optimist. I want it all." To which I would respond, you can have anything your heart desires, but you can't have *everything.* Realize that there simply isn't enough money or time to have and do everything in the world. Besides, if you did have it all, someone would invent something new, and you'd be behind until you had that too. Decisions must be made. Priorities must be set. My goal is to help you weed out those things that aren't priorities so you can pay yourself first and keep some of your economic power for your own benefit.

In the society we live in today mass marketers can pinpoint us with precision and, almost literally, *force* us to buy their products—some of which we don't even want. Think of all the advertising we're bombarded with every day, and if you don't believe you're affected, take another look. Why do you think advertisers display images that aren't even related to their product? They know they can link any feeling we want to their product and, like Pavlov's dog, we'll respond. There's only one reason advertisers spend billions of dollars on campaigns and pay ridiculous prices for thirty seconds during the Super Bowl: It works!

Complicating things is the instant-gratification syndrome. We want it *now*, and sometimes even now is too long to wait. Marketers have our number, and they can give us the feelings we want *now* if we'd just buy their products. On the other hand, saving and investing for worthy goals tends to come under the heading of "delayed gratification." It usually takes some time before you see the results, and that can be discouraging.

The reason writing down your expenses works so well is that you are consciously keeping your goals in front of you. By considering your financial goals on a regular basis, you get to experience them in your mind. In that sense, the gratification you get *is* immediate.

Let me ask an important question: *What would you do to become a millionaire?*

Most people can think of a lot of things they'd do—most of them difficult or undesirable. What if I told you that keeping track of your expenses habitually would make you a millionaire? Would you do it? I would hope so, but the sad truth is most people won't even make this simple effort. People want results without effort. You and I both know that's not how life works. With the addition of one important element (investing), becoming a millionaire is as simple as getting control of your expenses. Start by writing them down.

Let me give you an example:

What if every day you took the change in your pocket or a dollar bill and put it in a jar? Aside from those who are literally destitute, I don't know anyone who couldn't come up with a dollar a day. Anyway, let's say you decided to save that amount every day (about the price of a cup of coffee and a paper) and at the end of the month you took your $30, invested it (the way I'll show you later), and didn't touch your money.

The results are truly astounding. An eighteen-year-old who saves a dollar a day until he is sixty-five would eventually be worth several million dollars—even without doing anything unusual in the area of financial planning and investments. In fact, if he invests his daily dollar in a mutual fund earning 15 percent (and I can name many that have averaged better than that), the ultimate value of his investment would be *$2.65 million.* That's huge! Especially when you consider that this person has done nothing else to plan for his financial future.

In the example I've just cited, the out-of-pocket investment over the years was $17,000. Can you imagine the potential if the other 98 percent of the U.S. population began to practice this strategy on a consistent basis? Can you imagine the amount of growth and prosperity this country would experience? How many science and research jobs would be created? How much economic power we would be able to use positively? This simple concept is staggering, yet it's not conveyed in schools. The principle of compound interest is truly the eighth wonder of the world.

Now, you may say, "But, Tod, I'm already forty. For the last twenty-two years I haven't given a thought to saving. How can I possibly catch up?" Well, let me give you another example:

How many forty-year-olds do you know who could manage to cut a few cans of soda a day out of their diet and maybe a couple of steak dinners a month? Simple gestures like that would result in an average savings of $5 a day. Not everyone can pull this off, certainly. But anyone whose income approaches the median level—and who isn't totally addicted to sugar and fat—should be able to handle this easily.

The fact is, $5 a day invested the way I'll show you (assuming 15 percent return annually) over a twenty-five-year period would give you just over *$1 million.*

Read that again. It's mind-boggling when you think of the power of compound interest working in your favor instead of against you. I'm not talking about a major lifestyle change here, just $1 to $5 a day. In America we spend an average of $192 per person (nonsmokers and children included) per year on tobacco products. That's enough money that, if saved and invested, could make each of us wealthy in our lifetime. So, if you smoke, even though it doesn't seem like a huge cost, just cutting that out could make a major difference in your financial future. You must understand: If you aren't already saving enough for yourself and your family, you *could* be if you'd be just a little more watchful of where your money goes.

In some circles, budgeting is a plan for the future—not a record of the past. I prefer to keep track of my expenses as I spend, rather than plan a budget out to the year 2010. That just feels too constraining. I call my as-you-spend record keeping "take-control budgeting" and recommend it over forward-planning your expenses. I think there are just too many variables in our spending patterns to plan our future expenditures to the dollar. Furthermore, I think that most people find the money to buy the things they really want or need, so the goal here is to be aware enough of your cash flow to spend money only on things you really want. This awareness is accomplished by prioritizing your expenditures, which will be explained shortly. I think you'll find, as I did, that if you just keep a record of your prioritized expenses and balance them every month against your income, you'll instinctively know what to do next.

There are five steps to successful take-control budgeting:

1. Calculate your total income.
2. Choose your expense categories.
3. Set your budget amounts.
4. Write it down—control the outgo.
5. Prioritize your expenditures as you go (A, B, C, D).

The sample budget organizer that follows helps make all this clear. You'll find blank forms (Exhibit 1) in the back of this book.

First, calculate your total monthly income (or yearly salary and divide by twelve) and write the number in the appropriate monthly box at the top of the organizer. I always use my after-tax income for this figure. For most people, each month's income is the same. If your income varies month to month or you're on an unusual pay schedule, it may help to average, or "smooth out," your income numbers and make each month the same if your expenses are consistent month to month. Some evaluate their expenses on a weekly or quarterly basis.

MONTHLY EXPENSE ORGANIZER

	Budget	JAN.	FEB.	MAR.	APR.	MAY	JUNE	JULY	AUG.	SEP.	OCT.	NOV.	DEC.
Monthly Income (after deductions)		$3,000	$3,000	$3,000	$3,000	$3,000	$3,000	$3,000	$3,000	$3,000	$3,000	$3,000	$3,000
Expense Categories	Budget	$3,000	$3,000	$3,000	$3,000	$3,000	$3,000	$3,000	$3,000	$3,000	$3,000	$3,000	$3,000
Automobile	$400	$600											
Business	$300	$300											
Entertainment	$300	$300											
Groceries	$200	$200											
Miscellaneous	$200	$200											
Mortgage	$700	$700											
Personal	$400	$400											
Savings	$300	$300											
Utilities	$200	$200											
Total Monthly Expenses	$3,000	$3,200											
Monthly Balance	$0	–$200											

> **I am indeed rich, since my income is superior to my expense, and my expense is equal to my wishes.**
>
> —EDWARD GIBBON

I've found it works for me to just sit down once a month and reconcile my organizer. Make copies of this organizer and put it in a binder if you wish to keep records by year.

Second, choose your expense categories and list them down the left-hand column. Listed below are a few common expense categories.

Allowance/cash	Home repair/improvement
Automobile	Insurance
Business/travel	Interest expense
Child care	Medical
Children	Miscellaneous expenses
Clothing	Mortgage
Consumer debt	Personal
★ Contributions	Pets
Dry cleaning	Publications
Eating out	Rent
Entertainment	★ Savings/investment
Family advancement	Telephone
Gifts	Transportation
Groceries/supplies	Utilities
Health/fitness	Vacation

These are just examples. I don't know anyone who can keep up with all of them. Pick a few that fit your spending patterns (a quick view of your checkbook register or bank statement will help), and write them down in the left-hand column. Make sure you're practical, tailoring these categories to your own preference. For example, I lump all my common expenses into one "utilities" category—telephone, cellular telephone, electric, and water—because I've found that the fewer categories I try to keep up with, the better. Also, my wife and I have created a "health/fitness" category that includes everything from hair care to health club memberships. You may need to create some new categories for yourself. One word of advice: Try to stay out of the "miscellaneous" category as much as possible. It's better to lump things into a usable category than just label them "Misc." The first month I kept an organizer I made this mistake, and the "Misc." category wound up being larger than all the others. You want to know exactly where your hard-earned money goes.

The third step to take-control budgeting is to set your budget amounts and write them in the appropriate columns next to the categories you've labeled. Again, looking at your bank statement or check register should give you an idea where to start. You know your rent or mortgage payment, you know your car payment and insurance, but other categories may be hard to pinpoint. Write in some reasonable numbers and then play with them for a few months until you know your spending patterns in each area.

The fourth step, of course, is to write it down. A sample daily expense form follows. There's also a blank form (Exhibit 2) at the back of the book.

DAILY EXPENSE FORM

DATE	AMOUNT	CATEGORY	TYPE	PRIORITY
1/1	$600	AUTO	AX	A
1/1	$25	AUTO–GAS	CASH	A
1/1	$30	MISC.	CASH	C or D

This is where the habit of controlling the outgo is developed. At first, don't be surprised if this self-monitoring process is a little awkward; soon it will become as habitual as brushing your teeth. Make copies of this form if you like, or just use a notepad. For a long time I used a spiral notepad and just wrote the date at the top of each page. Now I have a place for my expenses in my daily planner/journal. It's been reported that Andy Warhol wrote his expenses down to the penny in his diary. I always round mine to the nearest dollar—but use whatever works for you. You can carry a notepad around or just keep receipts and write them down when you get home. The method you should use is one that insures you'll consistently follow through. Give this an honest effort.

"Character," it's been said, is the ability to carry out a worthy decision after the emotion of making the commitment has passed. Make a commitment to yourself to try this for three months and judge by results. You don't have to use my system—there are plenty of them out there (or you can develop your own). But find some way to take control in this area once and for all. The key to getting the results you want is consistency. There are millions of happy, wealthy, successful people in this country who've made controlling their expenses a part their daily routine. Start by writing it down.

The fifth and final step is to prioritize your expenses as you go. This in effect prioritizes your wants and helps you focus on the things you truly desire.

Let me give you an example. As a young man just entering the business world, I developed a strong desire for a particular suit that would "make" my professional wardrobe. It was a deep blue, double-breasted Armani—and needless to say, very expensive. Unfortunately, my fiscally conservative background made it hard to rationalize such a purchase. My family and friends had never considered owning top-of-the-line apparel an "A" priority. However, purchasing such a suit eventually became an A priority for me because dressing profession-ally at my place of business emerged as an important issue. Obviously, A priorities vary among people. They're as multiple and different as people are. It's not so important what you designate your A priorities as it is that you make controlled decisions.

The best way to prioritize your expenses, I think, is to do it as the money is spent. Then you can set realistic goals for future purchases. Whenever you record your expenditures on the daily expense form, write an A, B, C, or D next to each expense. I don't normally carry over these priority notations to the monthly organizer.

Use the following expense-priority definitions as a guide.

A   Necessary (groceries, rent, gas, savings, etc.)
B   Important (clothes, gifts, health club dues, etc.)
C   Nice (dining out, car detailing, trips, etc.)
D   Worthless (impulse purchases, stuff, etc.)

D-priority items are usually knickknacks, sale items you just can't resist, or things you see in the checkout line. Just for fun I've listed a few things that I consider D priority. I've also listed a brief description of these items, their "garage-sale value," and the future value of the cash had I saved and invested it for the next twenty years. This isn't a scientific study—just an example of an overactive imagination. Some of these "important" items I own and some I've talked myself out of. Some improve the quality of my life; most don't. To avoid embarrassment, I'll allow you to decide which is which.

ITEM/DESCRIPTION	GARAGE-SALE VALUE
Suedelike moccasins (made in Korea)	.25
Australian-outback cowboy hat (wisely purchased after rodeo and worn proudly on seven-minute drive home)	$ 2.00
Porcelain Statue of Liberty	.25
Deluxe Caribbean snorkeling set (works well in pool at home)	$1.00
Inflatable one-person catamaran	$5.00 to right buyer
Professional bocce set (still in package)	$2.00
"Whatever it takes" motivational mug-and-coaster set	$1.50
142-piece professional paintbrush set	$1.50
Aqua Sound III music belt (a comfortable, sensible, waterproof housing for radio and cassette players. It's designed for all active water sports— great for hot tubs too. It even floats!) I'm still living this one down	.50

Adjustable snow-tire chains (great in South Texas blizzards)	.00
Two-piece ceramic pig cookie jar (would look ideal if we had farm-animals glassware—not!)	.50
Climbometer (breakthrough-technology dual-gauged climbometer makes driving any Jeep loads of fun by showing you, through the marvelous "minifloating Jeep bubble-level concept," the angle of any hill that you're on. Backlit for easy reading at night, and installation is simple with self-adhesive backing and mounting bracket included. My personal favorite. Permanently attached to Jeep and is sure to accelerate depreciation of vehicle.)	($100.00)

I admit it! I had a little too much fun researching this example. I also ran a quick ballpark calculation taking the retail prices (probably close to $1,000) of these items and guesstimating their value in cash, if invested instead, in twenty years. The grand total, doubling my money about every five years (using the Rule of 72 and a 15 percent return, which we'll discuss later), in the year 2013: $16,000.

I'm not saying don't buy fun things. My point is, if you're not saving enough for your future, you can probably find the money by paying a little more attention to your expenses, especially your D priorities.

The most important reason to prioritize your expenses is to know where you spend unnecessarily on C and D items so you can begin thinking through each purchase more carefully, set goals, and really begin to get exactly what you want. In Part 3, we'll discuss planning your financial future. That may be a good place to set "want" goals and prioritize them. This book doesn't go into detail on setting and attaining specific material goals, but it may be a good idea to write down everything you want in a special "goals"

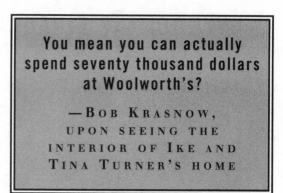

You mean you can actually spend seventy thousand dollars at Woolworth's?

—BOB KRASNOW, UPON SEEING THE INTERIOR OF IKE AND TINA TURNER'S HOME

notebook and prioritize each item. You'll be surprised how quickly you gravitate toward achieving them.

I always go one step further in my goal-setting sessions and give each item a definite time limit. Every personal-achievement expert I've ever conferred with emphasizes the importance of setting a specific date for the completion of a goal. I've found this works remarkably well. If you don't already consistently set goals and give them a time frame, you should develop the habit *now*.

Finally, once a month, add up your daily expenses from your daily expense forms or notebook and post them in the appropriate expense category in your monthly expense organizer. In the past, I've even tried posting them at the end of each day and keeping a running total (in pencil) so I'm constantly aware of how close I am to my budgeted amount for the month. I just add my categorized expenses in my daily expense form to the total amount of each category in my monthly organizer. I erase the old total and add my new total to keep my running balance current. It's relatively simple, since I have only a few entries a day and only a few categories are affected.

At the end of each month I add up each category and compare the totals to the budgeted amount. I can then adjust my budget or my spending habits to meet my plan. One other tip: For other tracking purposes, I always note in my daily expense form the type of payment I made (American Express—AX; personal check—CK; MasterCard—M/C; and so forth). If it helps, you can record that information in your monthly organizer as well.

OVERCOMING FINANCIAL FEARS

Money is an emotionally charged issue. At first glance, that doesn't seem logical—money is expressed in numerical terms, and numbers aren't emotional. They can be added, subtracted, multiplied, and divided. If you give the matter some thought, though, you realize the deep-seated beliefs—and corresponding emotions—we all have about what it means to have money. For example, some people believe that being poor signifies nobility and being rich signifies evil and selfishness. You and I know that nothing is further from the truth. Charity and good humor cut across economic lines, just as depravity does. Too, it's impossible to come up with an absolute definition of the minimum amount of money a person must have to be rich. A teenager can have $100 in his pocket and feel incredible while a real estate tycoon can be worth millions and feel strapped trying to take care of his overhead. In his novel *Texas* James Michener offers his version of the various gradations of wealth:

$1 million to $20 million	Comfortable
$20 million to $50 million	Well-to-do
$50 million to $500 million	Rich
$500 million to $1 billion	Big rich
$1 billion to $5 billion	Texas rich

In Texas, I've heard $100 million referred to as a "unit" as if to suggest that it's a starting place. The point is, it's not important what your goal is or how much you have, but that you choose to use your power in a positive way. By enjoying the process of accumulating wealth and sharing your good fortune, you "feel" wealthy.

Any time we try to change our situation, we experience fear. Sometimes that fear becomes so profound that we become immobilized. It's important that this paralyzing fear be handled immediately and not become ingrained. As Patrick Swayze's character says in the movie *Point Break*, "Fear causes hesitation, and hesitation will cause your worst fears to come true."

In the area of wealth accumulation, the fear of change is particularly acute. It's natural that the prospect of grappling with an unknown set of circumstances may cause some anxiety. As the saying goes, the only person who looks forward to change is a baby with a wet diaper. Still, we must be mindful of General Douglas MacArthur's dictum: "There is no security on this earth, there is only opportunity." Wanting total and absolute security yet fearing any form of change is disastrous to your financial health. In this age we live in, change is everywhere. If we don't adapt, we'll get run over. And, in any event, a world without change is a world without growth. If you don't expose yourself to new challenges, virtually every part of your life will remain static.

True, to risk change is to risk failure. But what must be always kept in mind is that each failure offers up a kernel of wisdom, which is why the world's most successful—and richest—people have invariably failed more than ordinary folks. Indeed, it is repeated failure—particularly in financial areas—that gives the wealthy a reservoir of wisdom to succeed.

One way to increase your odds of success is to anticipate changes in advance. More money inevitably brings greater responsibility and a wider range of choices. You must expect these kinds of choices to present themselves and decide how you're going to handle them. See yourself as you would like to be—not as you are. *See yourself wealthy, see the rewards, costs, and problems, and realize that you can handle them.* When it comes to saving and investing, people fear making a mistake and losing money, or worse, looking stupid trying. The truth is, you're going to make mistakes, some of them costly, but what's the cost if you don't even try? You must realize that *the only way to truly fail is to quit.*

I keep a quote in my planner that I think says it all. I hope you see as much value in it as I do:

> *Far better is to dare mighty things, to win glorious triumphs, even though checkered by failure, than take rank with those poor spirits who neither enjoy much nor suffer much, because they live in the gray twilight that knows not victory nor defeat.*

> —THEODORE ROOSEVELT

PART 2

ACTIVE WEALTH CREATION

WEALTH RITUAL 2

**Seek Your Dream—
If You Do What You Love,
the Money Will Follow**

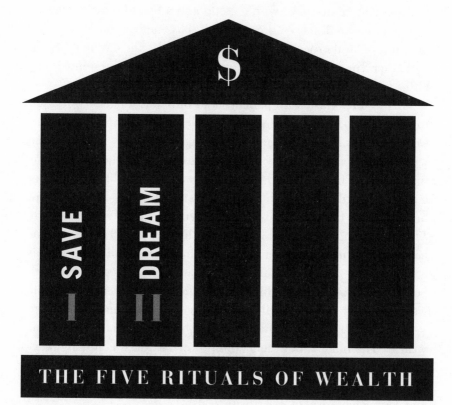

> **A musician must make music, an artist must paint, a poet must write, if he is to be ultimately at peace with himself.**
>
> —ABRAHAM MASLOW

A PERSON MIGHT HAVE CRINGED watching Pablo Casals conduct his daily routine. He was ninety years of age, and his arthritis caused him to walk laboriously, with a stoop and a feeble shuffle. He was frail and too tired to even dress himself. His emphysema made every breath a painful ordeal. It was saddening to see the old man beaten by Father Time this way. Pablo Casals, one of the greatest musicians of the twentieth century, was a sight to be pitied.

Before breakfast, with patience and difficulty, he moved himself to the piano bench—the first act of each of his mornings. Norman Cousins in his book *Anatomy of an Illness* describes what happened when Casals's clenched, swollen hands softly found the piano. "The fingers slowly unlocked and reached toward the keys like the buds of a plant toward the sunlight. His back straightened. He seemed to breathe more freely." Casals began playing Bach's *Wohltemperierte Klavier*, gaining strength and passion with every bar. "He hummed as he played, then said that Bach spoke to him here—and he placed his hand over his heart." Casals then played a Brahms concerto with power, grace, and control. In love with the music—his art—his body was transformed. He was filled with intense feeling and inspiration, and his body resembled that of a healthy, strong pianist. Cousins writes: "His fingers, now agile and powerful, raced across the keyboard with dazzling speed. His entire body seemed fused with the music; it was no longer stiff and shrunken, but supple and graceful and completely freed of its arthritic coils."

Seeking your dream means knowing what your heart desires and continually moving toward your own personal self-expression. It means finding that thing that consumes you so completely that you can't help but achieve enormous success through love in action. It means increasingly conforming your goals to your life's purpose—eventually making them one.

Put another way, seeking your dream is discovering what you love so much that you'd do it for free. When you identify whatever that is, and do it well and with passion and commitment, the world responds like you've never imagined.

The creation of wealth has two avenues. In this book you'll be learning two different yet parallel and complementary methods of accumulating a personal fortune—*active* and *passive*. Ritual 2 is active—building wealth by using only your personal resources. Rituals 3 and 4 are passive—getting your money to work for you while you sleep.

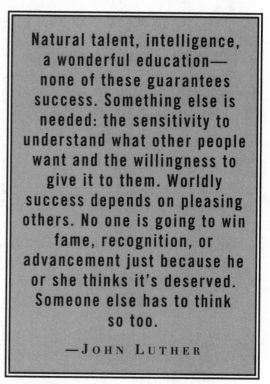

Natural talent, intelligence, a wonderful education—none of these guarantees success. Something else is needed: the sensitivity to understand what other people want and the willingness to give it to them. Worldly success depends on pleasing others. No one is going to win fame, recognition, or advancement just because he or she thinks it's deserved. Someone else has to think so too.

—JOHN LUTHER

Most people assume that, if they're to create wealth for themselves and their family, they must do it through the medium of *work*. While it's true that acquiring anything in life requires some physical or mental labor, the notion that you have to work your fingers to the bone is incorrect. By reading this book you'll learn how to create an abundance of wealth by following your heart and fulfilling your destiny in a way that's exciting and fun. We may not all be musicians, athletes, or movie stars, but I believe we all have a unique and special talent—something to offer humanity, something that makes us stand out. *Our mission in life is to find that "something."* If you really don't believe that creating tremendous wealth is as easy as finding what you love and having fun expressing yourself in your own way, listen up, because this discussion could change your life forever.

I've developed a personal philosophy about work and money: Money itself is not good or bad, it's simply a measure of energy—of some created value that other people are willing to pay for. When earned honestly and fairly, money is a measure of the intensity of the

> **When you are making a success of something, it's not work. It's a way of life. You enjoy yourself because you are making your contribution to the world.**
>
> —ANDY GRANATELLI

effort you give of yourself: It flows to you in direct proportion to the *quality* and *quantity* of the impact you've had on others. For example, a surgeon may earn the same income for a ten-hour lifesaving surgery that a rock musician earns for a two-song television appearance. The surgeon clearly has *quality* impact on his patient, while the musician's impact, although certainly containing a measure of quality, is weighted more toward *quantity*. The musician reaches a great number of people with a message that, while potentially moving, may not be life or death, like the surgeon's operation.

The lesson of this example is that you must find something to pursue that either allows you to have tremendous impact on a single individual *or* that you can bring to a multitude. Only by selecting one of these routes will you be well rewarded for your efforts.

The dictionary defines *work* as "strenuous activity that involves difficulty and effort and usually affords no pleasure." If that sounds awful, listen to its synonyms: *drudgery, toil, labor, task, chore, exertion, grind, slavery, plugging away, sweat, bullwork*, and *donkeywork*. Not too inspiring, huh? I don't believe this popular idea of work brings out the best in people. In fact, I think that it actually robs millions of people of their dignity and, ultimately, the most important years of their lives. People sometimes give up vital things like family, travel, and health for the sake of earning a living. And they do it because they feel like there are no other options.

The fact is, even if you win the rat race, you're still a rat! I don't care how many cars or homes you have, or how many zeros your paycheck has in it, if you're doing something you merely tolerate (or maybe even hate) for the sake of earning a living, you're still living at a subsistence level. Please don't misunderstand me: I'm not saying that you should do only what you *feel* like doing at the moment. Even among people who love their work, nobody wakes up every single day saying, "Gee, I just can't wait to get to work for the thousandth time on that project I've committed myself to." Everyone experiences a little resistance now and then, and we all have to learn self-discipline. Even the most creative, unpredictable musician, for example, has to go on the road once in a while and pay the bills. But if you're involved in work you love, your commitment to it and to yourself helps keep you on track. As actress Katharine Hepburn once said: "Life is to be lived. If you have to support yourself, you had bloody well better find some way that's going to be interesting."

To be everything we're capable of being and see the financial results we deserve, we must discover our *lifework*. I define *lifework* as "a mission of vision, purpose, and opportunity." That sounds a great deal more exciting than the traditional definition of *work*, doesn't it? In the pages that follow we're going to find out where your heart lies, what your lifework is, and how to use it to allow yourself to be pulled toward your dreams with everything you've got.

The first step begins with absorbing Wealth Ritual 2: **Seek your dream; if you do what you love, the money will follow.**

This ritual is best described in terms of the following five-step formula:

THE FIVE D'S OF PROSPERITY

1. Discover
2. Dream
3. Decide
4. Do It
5. Direct

1. DISCOVER WHO YOU ARE

For the next minute or so, forget about earning money and think about who you are. You might say, "What does who I am have to do with increasing my income?" Well, the fact is, if you want five times the income, you've got to be five times the person. The good news is that just being yourself is enough. The problem is that most people have lost that fire and enthusiasm that is a large part of their makeup. Consequently they aren't achieving the results they deserve.

The first step is to discover who you are deep down—what drives you. What are your needs and values? Do you need acceptance, support, safety, love? Do you value achievement, adventure, freedom, family, health? If all of your wants and needs were taken care of and you

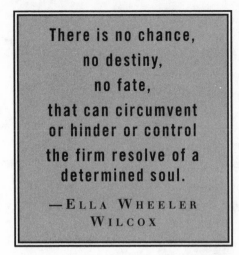

could just be yourself, what values would you consistently try to live by? Where would you spend most of your time, and with whom? What really motivates you? What is it that's most important to you?

When I ask people what motivates them, I often hear: "Well, Tod, I know what makes me tick— I'm *money*-motivated." To which I invariably respond: "No, no, it's not the money you want—it's the end result. You want security, freedom, power, or whatever it is that you think money will give you. The way to inspire and motivate yourself is to chase that end value—the one that's really important to you. If you do, you'll be living out your highest purpose and you won't have to look for the money, it will find you."

I contend that we should stop pursuing *only* the almighty dollar and spend some time pursuing ourselves and what we really want. That's the secret of living abundantly. As Alex Haley says in his novel *Roots*: "You can never enslave somebody who knows who he is." The concept of following your one and true nature is ancient. Socrates, in 400 B.C., felt that the key to human advancement was to know thyself. And Abraham Maslow, in the early 1900s, felt that the drive for self-actualization (becoming everything we're capable of becoming) is the most powerful force on the planet, if we can only understand ourselves enough to use it.

To be the best we can be, we can't just force ourselves to be disciplined and grind through activities we dislike; we must discover our deeper purpose in our life and our work. Think of what could happen in your professional and private lives if you were totally in charge of your future and were in a position to earn a fortune from something that is an almost effortless extension of your talents and abilities—something that has meaning and purpose. That's powerful!

A key to putting yourself in the financial driver's seat is to *make your life congruent—to align your life with your values.* If you're trying to spend more time at the office to make more money but one of your highest values is family and you'll have to be away from them more and more to succeed, you'll experience a clash in values. That is, two important values you hold—family and success—are competing for the same resources. Unless you truly feel that providing for your family is the best way to show you care about them, and they agree, you won't be happy. Companies are beginning to understand this. More flexible work schedules and mobile workplaces have become a reality. A lot of writers, consultants, and businesspeople now work out of their homes or mobile offices and are becoming more effective because the walls between the various compartments of their life have been broken down.

To discover your individual values, try answering the following question: What ingredients are essential for a meaningful life? The checklist below hints at the universe of possibilities. Which of these items do *you* find essential?

☐ Freedom	☐ Adventure	☐ Beauty
☐ Love	☐ Happiness	☐ Humor
☐ Excitement	☐ Courage	☐ Independence
☐ Security	☐ Learning	☐ Confidence
☐ Health	☐ Growing	☐ Fulfillment
☐ Passion	☐ Creativity	☐ Self-Expression
☐ Honesty	☐ Resourcefulness	☐ Communication
☐ Integrity	☐ Power	☐ Emotional connection
☐ Making a difference	☐ Family connection	☐ Acceptance/
☐ Intelligence	☐ Respect	Acknowledgment
☐ Being the best	☐ Support	☐ Spiritual connection
☐ Fun	☐ Challenge	
Others:		

When I reviewed a list like this for the first time, I thought it would be easy to pick the most important. I mean, doesn't everyone agree on what's truly essential in life? The answer is emphatically, no! To prove just how different we really are, try asking your spouse or a friend to review this list as well. You'll be amazed at how much different his or her list will be from yours.

You can learn an unbelievable amount about people just by asking a few questions about their values. Their answers reveal their deepest needs as human beings. And that type of information can be extremely useful both in business and in private life. In business, knowing what people truly value means not having to break down false barriers. By making it clear what your customer's most important need is, you can focus on how your product can satisfy it. In relationships, understanding what your partner or friend values helps strengthen the bond between you. You may even discover something about them that they themselves may not be aware of.

Acting in accordance with people's values may sound like manipulation, but it's not. There's absolutely nothing wrong with wanting to help other people fill their needs. That's how we provide useful service to others and, in the process, create wealth.

At this point in the book what I'd like you to do is to single out five values that are so meaningful and important to you that they've actually become *needs*. Refer back to the list of values, focusing on the ones that you checked off as important, and match the following statement with each: *"Life has absolutely no meaning without* _____*."* Is the item you're looking at a plausible blank filler? Do this over and over until you have five that are more important than any of the others. Write them down. Then pick one that is more meaningful than *all* others.

This paramount value has probably had more effect on your outlook and your actions than anything else in your life. I think you'll find that most of your behaviors in the past have been unconsciously moving you toward the five *needs/values* you selected, and the paramount one in particular. Please take a few minutes to review your five highest needs/values in their proper order:

NEEDS/VALUES

1. _____

2. _____

3. _____

4. _____

5. _____

This is not just a list of compelling words. Taken as an aggregate, these words, your top five values, are the blueprint of your behavior.

If you think about them for a moment, you'll probably realize that they've played an important role in the decisions you've made in the past and that they still affect your life today.

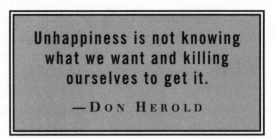

Unhappiness is not knowing what we want and killing ourselves to get it.

—Don Herold

They've guided you to the spouse and friends you have, the career you've chosen, the community in which you live—maybe even to the car you drive.

If you value family above all else, you've probably turned down opportunities to move away from your hometown. Or if you did move, you got homesick and your phone bill is outrageous. If you value achievement above all else, and were faced with the same decision of moving to a new city for a better job opportunity, you probably went for it. And if you value family and achievement equally, you know what a struggle it was to make that decision when your highest values clashed. If you value adventure highly, one might guess that you'd find appealing a long motorcycle ride across the country, or a hiking vacation. If health rates high on your list, it's easy to guess about your diet and workout habits.

I could go on and on. The point is, *power comes from knowing your highest values and making choices based on them rather than unconsciously being pulled toward them without ever knowing why.*

Of course, it's one thing to know things about yourself. It's another to use the knowledge to create enormous wealth and happiness.

No tool is more potent in the creation of success than *definiteness of purpose.* In fact, it's an absolutely crucial ingredient for achieving the level of financial rewards that most people only dream about. A purpose is simply a statement of resolution and determination about what is most important to you. And it doesn't happen accidentally—it's an intentional declaration of the person you want to be. It's a statement of what you want your place in history to be, and it always encompasses your highest values. It's an announcement of your commitment to a specific end.

Most people spend their lives floating around aimlessly because they haven't given any thought to who they are and what their purpose is. And we all know what happens to those of us who fail to decide our destinies for ourselves: We end up following someone else's plan for us, conforming our lives to the purpose of others. We become a tool to help other people realize *their* dreams.

Sometimes that's not bad—*if* you subscribe to the purpose that has been picked out for you. If, for example, you work for a company whose purpose and mission meshes closely with your own, that's fine. However, if you don't agree with your company's values, purpose, and mission, your life can be very painful—both mentally and financially.

My idea of having a purpose isn't about being a rebel. Rather, it's about allowing yourself the opportunity to plan in advance the meaning your life will take on. As I said earlier, a purpose is intentional. It's by design—your design. After all, who is more qualified to decide your place in this world than you? The people we think of as "winners" don't rely on luck or other people to tell them what mold they should fit into; they rely on themselves to go out and make it happen. Down through the ages, great thinkers have always stressed the importance of purpose. Ralph Waldo Emerson, the nineteenth-century essayist, wrote, "Luck is another name for tenacity of purpose." Michel de Montaigne, the most widely read European writer of the French Renaissance, stated, "The great and glorious masterpiece of a man is to know how to live on purpose." Writer Washington Irving once commented, "Great minds have purposes, others have wishes."

Haven't you ever wished you had just a little more conviction, a little more certainty, a little more confidence, in some area you were pursuing? Haven't you seen people who, seemingly against all odds, rose up and claimed their moment in time? Haven't you noticed that the most successful people in the world aren't necessarily the brightest, best-looking, best-educated, or most talented? The reason these people (some of them, to all appearances, quite ordinary) defy all odds and achieve the seemingly impossible is because deep down they have an unswerving faith and conviction in their abilities to carry out the task at hand. More important, *they believe without a doubt that all of their blood, sweat, and tears are meaningful.* All great figures in history believed at the deepest level that their actions and achievements served some grand and unique purpose. Whether they were serving their family, their company, or their country, they all had at their disposal the most powerful motivating force on the planet: purpose.

Certainly, your life's purpose can change, just like everything else that's important to you. We've all held beliefs and values that we can't believe were so important to us way back when. The point is: *You are in charge—not someone who doesn't know the quality or depth of your spirit and vision.* You may find, in a few years, that your outlook and dreams have changed, but when that moment comes, the decision about what to do next will be yours and yours alone.

Before presenting an exercise that will teach you how to create your own statement of ultimate purpose, let me share with you my own statement. I've written it in my planner, and I repeat it several times daily, even though I long ago committed it to memory. See if you can pick out my highest values.

PURPOSE STATEMENT: TOD BARNHART

I know that the purpose of my life is to be loving, compassionate, courageous, and fun; to move people and have tremendous impact in others' lives; to enjoy myself and graciously accept total abundance in every area of my life. In short, to live boldly "in the zone."

Yours can be shorter or longer, it doesn't matter. Use the guidelines below to make sure all the ingredients are there, and *please* give this an honest effort. I know people whose purpose in life is to simply "be happy and have fun." Whatever you decide, just remember that this is *your* purpose statement, and it is not to be formed around the goals and expectations other people have for you, or what you think everyone else expects you to be. This is your personal declaration of who you are committed to being and how you want to be remembered. *It is your personal proclamation of the depth and direction of your character.*

General Norman Schwarzkopf has written that he would like his epitaph to read: "A good soldier who loved his family." Obviously, the general is a man who is in touch with his deepest self, who possesses clarity of purpose. All of us should aim just as high.

What I'd like you to do now is take your top five needs/values and consolidate them in a purpose statement. Here are some guidelines:

THE RULES

1: It must begin with "I, [state your name], know that the purpose of my life is to:"

2: It must include all of your top five needs/values. You don't necessarily have to use each exact word, as long as the equivalent meaning is there.

3: It must be specific in terms of values and actions defined but not in terms of money or rewards. (For example, avoid phrases like "to make a million dollars" or "to be the world's greatest harmonica player." Those aren't values, but rather, goals, which we'll define later.) The idea is to develop a purpose statement that is achievable, whether the world rewards you or not.

4: It must be general enough for you to experience it, on some level, just about every day.

5: You must spend at least fifteen to thirty minutes developing it. *Don't fall into the trap of thinking that you'll find time to design your life's purpose later.* After all, how much time have you found to devote to this area in the last twenty, thirty, or fifty years?

Okay, let's get busy. You may want to use some scrap paper for your initial ideas and then write your formal statement of purpose.

I, _____, know that the purpose of my life is to

Please make sure you put some thought into the development of this purpose statement. It doesn't have to be grammatically correct or even sensible to others, but it does have to come from your heart. It must be emotional—something that stirs you to act, not just an academic exercise.

When you're done, sit back for a second and ask yourself three short questions:

1. How does it feel to have a well-designed purpose for my life?
2. How will living "on purpose" affect my ultimate destiny?

3. How does it feel to be guided by a purpose of my own choosing, rather than following the plans of others?

Answering these questions should give you a feeling of certainty about your future, a feeling of confidence that you *will* realize your hopes and dreams.

And having met this precondition for lifelong success, you should use the momentum to define what it is you really want in life—to get a fix on your dream lifestyle. What kind of relationships do you want? What kind of income? Anything is possible, as long as you're willing to dedicate yourself to its achievement.

As Robert Kennedy once said: "Other men see things as they are and ask 'Why?' I see things that never were and ask 'Why not?'"

2. DREAM

Near Hoboken, New Jersey, 1939: A thin twenty-four-year-old kid with swept-back greasy hair waits tables at a roadhouse called the Rustic Cabin. Newly married and sharing a combined income of fifty dollars a week with his wife, Nancy, young Francis isn't exactly prosperous. Still, in the Depression, with 9.4 million Americans unemployed, he's happy to have any job at all. That—and a powerful dream—is what keeps his optimism high.

One evening Harry James, the famous trumpet player and band-leader, wanders into the Rustic Cabin. Seizing the moment, the boy-ish Francis suddenly takes off his apron and mounts the tabletop. As James would later put it: "He'd sang only eight bars when I felt the hairs on the back of my neck rising. I knew he was destined to be a great vocalist." Harry hires the young man as his band's featured male vocalist for seventy-five dollars a week, and the world soon comes to know Francis Albert Sinatra in a big way.

The secret to wealth in abundance is to never be afraid to throw your apron on the floor. Never be afraid to jump up on the table and sing!

This is where we find out what you're all about, what you stand for, and what turns you "on." This is where we ask and answer questions like: If you had all the time, capital, and freedom to choose anything you wanted, what would you do? What kind of lifestyle would you pursue to leave your mark? If there were no such thing as failure,

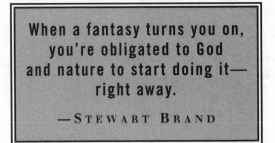

When a fantasy turns you on, you're obligated to God and nature to start doing it— right away.

—STEWART BRAND

what life experiences would you have? These types of questions will help lead you to your ultimate vision.

Think about our heroes— athletes, entertainers, famous entrepreneurs. Do they have nine-to-five jobs, or is their work an almost effortless expression of themselves? You know the answer. People don't want a job, they want an opportunity. A J.O.B. is just that: *just our bodies.* A job has nothing to do with creativity, imagination, inspiration, talent, enthusiasm—it's not something our heart connects with. That's why jobs pay lousy and most people can't use them as stepping stones to financial abundance, no matter how hard they try.

As seekers of wealth—and here I emphasize *active* wealth—we have two choices. We can either select an employment situation that permits self-expression, or we can change our present situation to enable self-expression to take place.

Let's begin by answering those key questions I alluded to above. I've listed them, in somewhat more elaborate form, below. Write at least a paragraph in response to each, then store them for future reference. It can be fun to refer back to them a few years from now, after you've achieved all your goals.

1: If you had all the time, capital, and freedom to choose anything you wanted, what would you do to leave your mark?

2: If there were no such thing as failure, what life experiences would you have?

3: If you won the lottery, would you go to work tomorrow? Would you stay at your same job? If not, what would you do? After you've achieved financial freedom, taken a vacation, and bought a few toys, what activities, charities, or businesses would you commit yourself to?

Answering these questions honestly will help you form an idea of what you want your life to be about. There really are very few constraints on what you can do. In today's world we really don't need to be worried about our basic needs, and people have made tremendous fortunes in areas that are probably a great deal sillier than your most unlikely dream. Why not go for it, and have the money too? What and who is keeping you from your destiny?

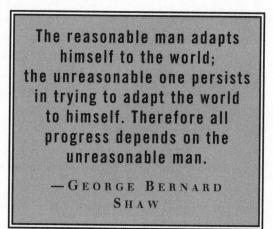

The reasonable man adapts himself to the world; the unreasonable one persists in trying to adapt the world to himself. Therefore all progress depends on the unreasonable man.

— GEORGE BERNARD SHAW

Crucial to achieving your vision is taking all the "wants" you have right now and making them "needs." The reason you don't have all the things you want in life is because they are just that: wants. In my studies of human achievement, I've found one thing to be absolutely true: *If we truly believe we deserve something, we somehow manage to get it.* We all believe we deserve food, clothing, shelter, and transportation. Because we view these items as needs, most of us experience them on a daily basis. However, we don't all agree that we deserve total abundance in every area of our lives, and our situations reflect that.

I believe that where relationships, health, and finances are concerned, we *deserve* abundance. But in order to claim it we can't just want and wish—we have to *need*. Only then will we be motivated to take action. After all, food itself isn't enough to nourish hunger. First, you have to get up and walk into the kitchen!

To help you formulate a set of actions that will enable your highest needs/values to pull you toward your desired outcome, I'd like you to list right now, next to your highest values, ten things you enjoy doing and ten ways you can make money. They can be things that will work in your present employment situation, or they can be ideas that are totally different from anything you've ever done before. Try to have fun with this. Don't worry if your ideas don't make sense, or if they don't seem possible right now—we'll thin them out later. This is a time to get creative and think like a kid again.

If you ask a kid how he's going to make his fortune, he'll probably say something like: "I want to drive a soda pop truck around like they do with ice cream trucks and sell sodas to people playing out-doors. That would be fun, plus you could have all the pop you want!" (I didn't just make that up—that was my dream job as a little kid.) To an adult such an idea seems silly. But really, what's so silly about it? Fortunes are being built on ideas no more elaborate than this every day.

Witness the success of "two of the slowest, chubbiest guys in the seventh grade," as Jerry Greenfield put it, who decided that few things in the world made them happier than ice cream. As adults, these two friends, armed with only a $5 investment in an ice cream–making correspondence course, opened a small ice cream store in Vermont. Amazingly, their concept exploded into a $58-mil-lion-plus enterprise, Ben & Jerry's. The two had no experience man-aging such a large "overnight success," but they found something they loved, and success followed.

So please, just let your imagination go and dream. Ask "what if?" It's the first step to achieving all that you long for.

The chart below gives you an idea what your worksheet should look like.

Value	Activities You Enjoy	Ways to Make Money
1. Health	Dancing Bike riding	Teach dance Sell restored bicycles Start bicycle-messenger service
2. Love	Weekend getaways Romance novels	Open bed & breakfast Run travel-arrangement service Write/edit/sell novels
3. Fun	Listening to music Going to concerts	Open rental and used CD store Teach adult music appreciation Do concert bookings/local bands
4. Adventure	Camping Fishing	Give guided tours Open outdoor-gear specialty store Design new lure/equipment
5. Making a difference	Teaching Working with children	Write children's books Tutor Invent new toy/tough clothes Open recreation/learning center

By the way, if you have trouble thinking of activities you enjoy, ask and answer this simple, fill-in-the-blank question for each value as you come to it: *I become so totally involved, I lose all track of time when I _____*. Whatever that blank is could be your key to financial success and happiness. For example, you may love to dance so much that every care you have in the world disappears when you're on the dance floor. If you value health or fitness highly, dancing (or teaching dancing) may be a good activity to put in that category. Again, these ideas can be compatible with your present occupation or something else entirely. Don't cheat yourself out of this powerful exercise.

Having taken some time to jot down ideas about how to make money, ask yourself a few questions:

1: What if I could earn a fortune by expanding some of the activities I already enjoy? How would that make me feel? How would that affect my outlook on life and others?

2: How would it feel to let go of old hang-ups and baggage I may have about work and money and begin in my own unique way to create the level of wealth I deserve?

3: How successful could I be if I could create wealth from activities related to things I really love? What could I create? What kind of an impact could I have?

These types of questions will help you realize that your dreams are really worth going for, and that you *can* have it all. In addition, by answering these questions you give your dreams validity and hope. You also begin to formulate a way to make them happen—a kind of preliminary plan. And once you begin to plan, you've already begun to accept the result as achievable and worthwhile.

Questions, it turns out, are amazing tools. They help us dream up and create any result we want. With a few simple questions you can take a vague idea, consider it a dream, pronounce it a vision, and mentally plot a course for its completion. *You can go from itch to rich by asking and answering questions that confirm the significance of your dreams.*

In the next section we'll be talking about how to make that leap from a dream to a vision. It starts with the power of *decision*.

3. DECIDE

In Tupelo, Mississippi, in the early 1950s it is a mark of success to find any type of skilled work. Elvis Aaron Presley knows the safest course of action is to follow through on his plan to become an electrician. Even so, he longs to become a musician. Elvis's father has strong opinions of his own, and he not-so-subtly makes sure the boy gets the message: "You should make up your mind—either about being an electrician or playing guitar. I never saw a guitar player that was worth a damn." The young man is forced to make the most critical decision of his life. He concedes that turning down a steady career seems foolish, but he's convinced he can turn his dream into reality.

We all know that Elvis became a legend. He was just a man, and he made mistakes like the rest of us. But behind the tragedy, one thing is certain: The man left his mark. He still has a cultlike following, and his burial site in Memphis has become a place of pilgrimage.

I can think of nothing that has more power than a well-made decision. It can create tremendous riches, joy, and happiness, whereas its counterpart, indecision, often creates worry, weakness, and failure. Difficult decisions invariably have the most impact on your life. As Napoleon said, "Nothing is more difficult, and therefore more precious, than the ability to decide."

In the next few pages you'll develop compelling reasons to decide to commit to your dreams. You'll uncover the *where* and *why*—where you're going and why it is so important that you go there and not let fear, or anything else, stand in your way.

When we talked about purpose we focused on ourselves—what we want to stand for and what we want our lives to be about. In the world of business, however, to achieve financial success we must focus on and fill the needs of others. For other people to see value in our product or service, it must meet *their* needs. Hence, it's important to develop a *lifework statement* that defines the benefits other people will derive from our efforts.

Before you construct your own lifework statement, it may be helpful to take a look at mine:

> **My lifework—my mission of vision, purpose, and opportunity—is to: Help people reach their financial dreams and elevate the quality of their lives.**

Please notice that my life-work definition is measured not in terms of numbers or income but in terms of service. It's not a goal, it's a mission statement—something

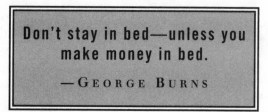

> **Don't stay in bed—unless you make money in bed.**
>
> —GEORGE BURNS

I've committed myself to regardless of the outcome. Goals are important, and we'll get to them. But a mission or lifework statement—well, that should be written in a way that allows you to achieve it every single day.

I know that even if I have a relatively slow day (slow for me is usually Mach 1), I can still accomplish my lifework by impacting a few people in a positive way. Living my lifework can encompass a variety of activities: writing, speaking, media tours, individual counseling, or just helping out a friend. That's what makes my lifework so enjoyable: It's not work—it's just me! I try to remember that I don't win by taking advantage of others and making a fortune. I win by helping other people fill their needs and get the good feelings they want about themselves.

Believe me, making people happy leads to wealth. Interview just a few very successful people, and you'll see what I mean.

Here are some guidelines for writing your lifework statement:

THE RULES

1: It must begin with "My lifework—my mission of vision, purpose, and opportunity—is to:"
2: It must focus on need(s) and/or value(s) of *other people* (health, success, financial dreams, etc.).
3: It must include an action on your part that defines broadly how you can serve others with your specific talents and abilities (i.e., to help others).
4: It must be totally congruent with your values. For example, if your highest value is health and you work as a salesperson for a cigarette company, you're likely to feel conflicted. If that's the case, and you aren't ready to change careers (which I'd strongly suggest), then you must redefine your role. A good statement—assuming that three of your highest values are friendship, efficiency, and service—might be: "My lifework—my mis-

sion of vision, purpose, and opportunity—is to service
my clients in a friendly, efficient manner." The point is
that you don't want to define yourself as someone whose
work goes against his core values. This creates misery
and leaves very little room for success. Your lifework
definition must be congruent with who you are so you
can effortlessly walk your talk.

A final point: Don't make this hard. You don't have to include all
of your values or all of the values and needs you service in your occupation. Just pick a few empowering words and develop a sentence or
phrase that is totally in line with your core beliefs and values—a
phrase that defines *what you do.*

When people ask me what I do, I say, reciting my lifework statement verbatim, "I help people reach their financial dreams and elevate
the quality of their lives." I may reword it if the situation calls for that.
Or I may lengthen and elaborate, going on to say, "I write, speak, and
counsel people in the area of financial self-improvement," explaining
further if it seems appropriate. You may eventually share your statement with other people, if you choose, but the point is to develop this
statement not for other people but for yourself. You want to define
beforehand exactly what you're going to say when you talk to yourself.
When you experience a moment of self-doubt, you can recite your purpose to yourself in a way that's positive, purposeful, and inspiring.

I once knew a car salesman who told me he "crammed cars down
people's throats," trying to force a sale when they came into the
showroom. What do you think he thought of himself and his profession? Do you think he saw himself as someone who helped others get
exactly what they wanted? How successful and happy do you think
he was? You know the answer.

*It's impossible to achieve long-term success unless you believe,
correctly, that you provide a valuable, needed product or service.* If
you don't provide value, you won't be in business very long.
Consumers aren't dumb. In fact, they're the smartest people in the
world when it comes to letting go of their hard-earned bucks.

The supersuccessful people in your industry or profession all
probably have only one common characteristic that separates them
from the crowd: a confident acceptance that the compensation they

receive is in direct proportion to the level of service they provide and the value they add. I applaud Tom Cruise for responding, when asked about his enormous income from making films: "If I wasn't worth it, they wouldn't pay it. And the day I'm not, they won't!"

Okay, it's time now to get out a piece of paper and define your own lifework.

Now that you've defined your lifework in positive, empowering terms, take a minute to ask and answer a few questions:

1: How do I feel about my career or job now that I have a well-designed lifework statement that expresses what's really in my heart and soul?

2: How will adopting this lifework affect my clients, coworkers, subordinates, and employer, and what implication does that have for my destiny?

3: How much more effective and fulfilled will I be now that I'm guided by my lifework?

In addition, I'm going to ask you to answer two more questions— the two most powerful in this book, designed to give you strong reasons to commit to your lifework. I'd like you to spend at least ten minutes thinking about your answers. One question is positive and one is negative, and together they are the carrot and the stick—the pleasure and the pain associated with this type of decision. The first helps you visualize all of the rewards that you'll receive if you do decide to make the work you've done here a consistent part of who you are. The second allows you to experience all of the frustration, disappointment, and pain of failing to make that decision. Answering both of these questions is necessary for change on a dramatic scale, and I know that's what you want, otherwise you wouldn't have bothered to follow me this far. *This is where you decide whether to follow your carefully designed lifework once and for all. This is where you decide whether to ever again accept less than you're capable of.* Please take the time to do this *now*.

On a sheet of paper, answer each of the following two questions with a one-paragraph response:

1: What are the rewards I will receive, now and in the future, by committing to and living by my highest values, my ultimate purpose, and my lifework statement? What will I experience emotionally, financially, and in terms of self-esteem, now and in the future, if I decide today?

2: What feelings will I experience, now and in the future, if I don't decide now? Where will I be financially, emotionally, and in terms of self-esteem, now and in the future, if I continue to put off this decision? Will I be more jaded and weak, or less? What will it cost me if I don't decide today?

I hope by now you've decided that there are just too many good things in life to wait any longer to commit to your dreams. And I hope you've realized that not deciding will be more painful than going for it. If you still aren't sure, let me ask you a few questions: *What if this could really make a difference in your life? What if you could make a few simple decisions today that would alter your destiny forever? Would you do it? Would you do it now?*

And if not now, when?

I once read a quote that took my life in a different direction:

> **There is only one success—to be able to spend your life in your own way.**
>
> **—CHRISTOPHER MORLEY**

I read that quote several times in that one sitting, and a light bulb went on in my head. "That's it!" I thought. Success isn't measured in numbers, or fame, or money—it's not a line drawn somewhere just above the million-dollar mark. Success is choosing your own destiny and living out your potential in your own way. Success is a journey, not a destination. Working hard in a job you hate, just for the money, is the farthest thing from success. True success is having the power to decide for yourself what it is you want, and then going for it, enjoying the process, not just the end result.

Too many people in our society don't know what they want and by default are forced into the rat race. The typical path is this: get out of school, take the highest-paying job offered, and affix a bumper sticker to their car that says, "I owe, I owe. It's off to work I go!" We work hard our whole career, put up with office politics we'd rather not be involved in so we can eventually be happily retired. The idea is to suffer for forty years in a "job" so we can be "happy" later.

Obviously, you don't want to take the typical path. To live life in your own way means to choose your own form of contribution through work—not being a slave to the grind.

After reading the Morley quote, I decided to always strive to live life in my own way. I chose to never accept blindly what was given, and to always look for ways to contribute to others and enjoy the journey of life. In a moment of inspiration I sat down and began to write. I thought of two neighbors who choose to look at life differently and consequently experience different outcomes in their lives. I visualized their two situations: one man is financially secure, confident, successful, and caring; the other, jaded, weak, broke, selfish, and uncaring. I named the two men, respectively, Arthur Peace and George Petty, and set about sketching them, asking myself which of them I was most like at this point and which of them I most wanted to emulate.

As you read the character sketches I wrote years ago, please ask yourself the same questions they ask themselves:

Arthur Peace lives his own way. This morning he wakes up early as usual—when the summer sun casts a ray across his face. He rises smiling. "Today is going to be a beautiful day," he thinks. He takes a quick glance in the mirror and likes what he sees. He stands upright, his straight, still-youthful posture conveying an air of confidence. He is happy, healthy, wealthy, successful, and deeply in love with his wife and family. He briefly thinks of some of the many friends and associates he's grown to know and love over the past fifty years. Staring at himself in the mirror again, he asks, "How is it I'm so fortunate? What can I do today to give something back to a world that's given so much to me? How can I show the people I care about that I appreciate them and am grateful for my good fortune?" He thinks of many answers and begins to plan his day around them. He starts with a morning jog on the beach, trying to clear his mind. But the thought remains, as it has for many years: I am truly the luckiest and happiest man alive.

George Petty leads a different life. He pounds the snooze button on his alarm in disgust. "Seven o'clock already," he moans. He scrambles to the shower—he can't be late for work—then rushes past the mirror without a glance. After all, who wants to see another gray hair or a new wrinkle? He dresses, grabs a doughnut on the way out to the car. "Out of my way," he yells as he fights the morning traffic. "I hate this drive!" He thinks back to only a few years ago when he shared this miserable drive with his neighbor, Arthur Peace. He can't believe Arthur is retired already. The company is even retaining him as a part-time consultant. "I make okay money. I'm pretty good at my job, and I can't even afford to take a vacation," he thinks. "George," he asks himself, "why weren't you born rich, talented, or lucky? Why does everybody else seem to get all the breaks? How much longer will I have to live like this? Why is life so unfair? I'll probably have to work till I drop and never get anywhere on this treadmill. Oh, well, maybe Social Security will take care of me if the kids can't."

Look to the future. Which will it be? George or Arthur? Unfortunately, most people are financially miserable. As I mentioned at the beginning of this book, 98 percent of Americans at or over the age of sixty-five are unable to support themselves! Many of them don't need just a little help, they are totally dependent on others. Why is it that 85 percent of the over-fifty crowd can't come up with $250 on their own after living full, usually productive lives? Conversely, why is it that some people are able to live the life of their dreams? *Are you willing to do what it takes to learn the answers to these questions? Are you willing to do what it takes to be financially free? Are you willing to discover and implement the consistent actions and thought patterns of the few who actually achieve financial independence?*

Most of America's senior citizens will live out their remaining years feeling like burdens to society. Will you become one of them? Now is the time to *decide*.

Recently, I came across this comment from a middle-aged executive: "It's too late. I've spent too many years doing exactly what was expected of me: being a good son, a good husband, a good father. In my company I'm known as a 'good soldier.' When I ask myself what I am about, I'd have to say I don't know anymore. I've tried for so long to fit in, I've held back for so long, I don't know what or who I am."

Let me tell you, it's better to decide sooner than later, but as long as we live, we have the gift of choice. *It's never too late to make the right decision.*

4. DO IT

During the 1957 World Series Henry "Hank" Aaron, who in later years would break the all-time home run record, marched purposefully toward home plate with bat in hand. He dug into the batter's box with his eyes fixed on the pitcher and his thoughts focused on the task at hand. Yankee catcher Yogi Berra noticed that Aaron grasped the bat the wrong way. "Turn it around," Berra said, "so you can see the trademark." But Aaron's eyes shifted only between the pitcher's mound and the outfield fence as he said: "Didn't come up here to read. Came up here to hit."

All of the most profound knowledge in the world is useless until someone takes action. So far we've dug deep into who you are and what's important to you. And we've dreamed about all of the good things your future holds. Now it's time to use those tools to create a road map of your destiny. It's time to put in motion a set of specific plans and actions that will pull you toward your dreams. As Saint Thomas Aquinas once said, "Three things are necessary for the salvation of man: to know what he ought to believe, to know what he ought to desire, and to know what he ought to do."

Before we create that road map, let me explain something. Many times we think that in order to take our performance to the next level we have to work harder. If we're in a slump, or stretching for a goal, we usually rearrange our schedule so we can put in more hours. We explain to our family that a certain amount of sacrifice will be necessary—perhaps a few nights a week, or a few Saturdays a month, away from home. Then we make lists and block out time meticulously so we can increase our output.

Now, that's not all bad, but the problem is this: We're assuming that it's possible to move to another level by using the same tools we've always used but for a longer duration. Unfortunately, that's not

> ## To avoid criticism, do nothing, say nothing, be nothing.
>
> —ELBERT HUBBARD

always the case. *Sometimes in order to move to a new level, we have to get new tools, new technology.* After all, man couldn't reach outer space until the rocket was invented. So, at times it makes sense to take a step back and look for assistance in a way that we haven't considered before. That's why I'm so big on values and purposes. Many people haven't given these topics much thought, but they're marvelous tools that can increase your results exponentially.

The answer isn't longer hours, it's more effective hours. If you don't constantly expand your "success toolbox," you'll eventually find that there simply aren't any more hours you can squeeze from a day. It's the equation of longer hours with increased success that causes many people to sacrifice virtually everything else in their lives for the sake of earning a living. Something has to give. And if you don't expand who you are, the things that "have to give" could be those that are really most important to you.

So, the key is to deepen ourselves, to have layers of tools and methods at our disposal, so we can continually produce more and more, with the same or less effort. *After all, the taller the building, the deeper and more complex the foundation.* The personal-development exercises in this section are designed to expand who you are and the foundational resources you have. By using these powerful tools of values, purpose, and lifework, you can more carefully direct your actions in a way that produces maximum results.

This next exercise we're going to do is designed to help you set goals and take action toward their achievement. In other words, to get you to *do it!* The first step is to follow the format of the "Values/Goals/Tasks" sheet on the following page and list your top five needs/values in the appropriate space. Then, for each value, refer back to the activities you enjoy doing that you listed in the exercise on page 72. Using these activities and your initial ideas of ways to make money in conjunction with your lifework statement, form a long-term goal that you'd love to achieve.

To illustrate, let's go back to a previously mentioned example. If you love to dance, value health and fitness highly, and think teaching

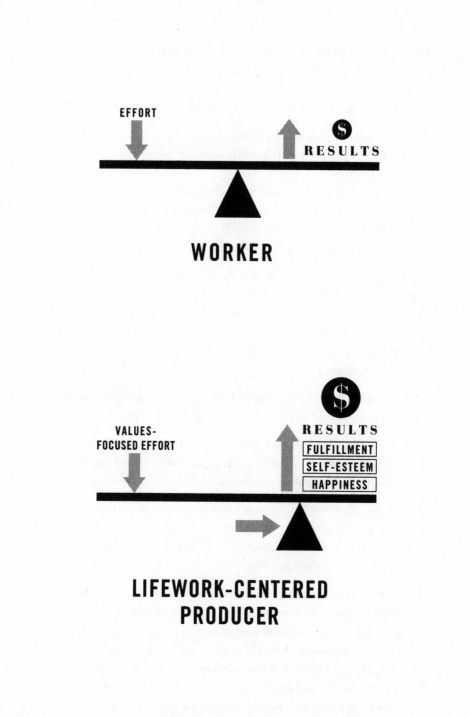

EFFORT

$ RESULTS

WORKER

$

VALUES-
FOCUSED EFFORT

RESULTS

FULFILLMENT
SELF-ESTEEM
HAPPINESS

LIFEWORK-CENTERED
PRODUCER

dance classes might be a fun way to make money, your long-term goal might be something like: to open up a small dance school within the next year.

And your daily, weekly tasks (or action list) might be something like:

1. Brush up on skills by taking two dance classes a month.
2. Interview one local dance instructor per month for helpful hints.
3. Take a small-business workshop to learn the basics.
4. Save $200 per week for initial start-up costs.
5. Send one mailing per month to prospective students, announcing the year-end grand opening.

You want to make sure that both your purpose and lifework statement fit closely with your goals. They won't be exact, but just make sure they support each other. Again, using the dance example, your purpose and lifework statement might be something like this (remember, the purpose statement primarily relates to self and the lifework statement primarily to others):

PURPOSE: I know that the purpose of my life is to constantly love, learn, and have fun, and help others do the same.

LIFEWORK: My lifework—my mission of vision, purpose, and opportunity—is to help those around me feel good about themselves and confident in their own abilities.

Finally, after listing each value and the corresponding goal and tasks, write at least a paragraph on why the goal is worth the time and effort involved in achieving it. Using the dance example, the answer might be something like:

I want to own my own business so I can have the freedom to enjoy my success. I'd like to help other people discover the joy of learning to dance. I can stay in shape by teaching regularly. My self-esteem will be improved by doing things I love and am good at, on a daily basis. I can feel satisfied that I have created a business that best represents who I am. My students will look up to me, and I can positively impact their lives.

Does this sound like a surefire formula for success? Absolutely! Structured in the above manner, this action plan can't help but pull this hypothetical person toward his or her dreams. So go ahead and try it yourself. Spend as much time as you need to complete this exercise. It will serve as your blueprint for success and financial abundance. (See chart, page 86.)

Now that you're done, how does it feel to have a carefully laid-out life plan that acknowledges your most important dreams and values? Pretty good, I'd guess. The most difficult part of chasing your dreams is completed. But you may wonder how you're going to pull it off. Believe me, the *why* comes first, the *how* comes later. As psychiatrist Victor Frankl, a Holocaust survivor, stated in his book *Man's Search for Meaning*, "A man who knows the *why* for his existence will be able to bear almost any *how*." If you can find enough compelling reasons to go for it, you'll find a way to make it happen.

5. DIRECT

In July of 1939, Douglas Corrigan, an American aviator piloting a Curtis-Robin monoplane, lifts off into the skies over New York City. His aircraft, nicknamed *Lizzy*, is ten years old and lacks a radio—or for that matter, any safety devices or beam finders. For his twenty-seven-hour trip to Los Angeles, he has added extra fuel tanks that completely obscure his forward view, so he is forced to look out the side windows to see where he's going. Just under twenty-four hours later, Corrigan and *Lizzy* land in Dublin, Ireland. Corrigan has somehow gotten turned around and flown completely across the Atlantic Ocean by mistake! Excitedly, he exclaims to airport officials, "I flew the wrong way!" Shortly after, he is dubbed "Wrong Way Corrigan"—the name by which history comes to know him.

All of the planning, effort, and achievement in the world won't get you the desired result if it's misdirected. *The last thing you want to do is spend your life climbing, scratching, and clawing your way up the ladder of success, only to come to the end of your life and realize the ladder was resting against the wrong wall.* This section is about continually taking inventory of where you are and where you're going—in other words, asking yourself why, at any given moment, you're choosing one path rather than another.

VALUE	LONG-TERM GOALS(S)	DAILY/WEEKLY TASKS
1.		

Why is achieving this goal worth the time and effort involved?

| 2. | | |

Why is achieving this goal worth the time and effort involved?

| 3. | | |

Why is achieving this goal worth the time and effort involved?

| 4. | | |

Why is achieving this goal worth the time and effort involved?

| 5. | | |

Why is achieving this goal, along with my other important ones, worth the time and effort involved?

This section is *not* about changing yourself and taking on a new identity every few months. It's about continually growing by adding layers to who you are and what you're about. It's about becoming comfortable with the idea of continual, gradual improvement and expansion, and understanding that such personal evolution must be monitored and directed on an ongoing basis. What I'm getting at here is the notion of *transformation*. As Thaddeus Golas, author of *The Lazy Man's Guide to Enlightenment*, has written, "The direction of change to seek is not in four dimensions: it is getting deeper into what you are, where you are, like turning up the volume on the amplifier."

Let's talk a little about one's personal code of conduct. All great people have certain standards by which they live, things they expect of themselves—a code. A code is the inherent or distinctive qualities to which a person is emotionally committed and that give that person character.

Even when you're living in a purposeful way and chasing your destiny, some days things just don't seem to work out perfectly. The key to staying on track when you feel like you might give up is taking pride in the things you *can* control. If every single day you live up to your own personal code, you can feel like a success even if the external rewards seem elusive. Regardless of the outcome, you've succeeded. And no one can ever take that away from you. Victor Frankl, who endured years of unspeakable horror in a Nazi death camp, expressed this point by quoting a German poet, *"Was Du erlebst, kann keine Macht der Welt Dir rauben."* ("What you have experienced, no power on earth can take from you.")

I guess you could say that a personal code is a way of measuring yourself. Not by the numbers and the accomplishments for which the world will recognize you, but by your own personal idea of what it takes to be the best you can be. If every single day you strive to be your best, your confidence and self-esteem will build. And if every day you succeed in living by your own high standards, you'll develop a pattern of success and condition yourself positively.

Think about it: *What kind of power and confidence would you have if every day of your life you won in some way? What would that do for your resolve, your spirit? How would that affect your destiny?*

You know the answer: You'd begin to see yourself as a capable, successful person, a winner, and the rewards would follow.

Ben Franklin had a code that he tried to live by every day. He called it his *list of virtues*, but it can also be thought of as a list of values. Every single day he tried to live strictly by every virtue in his code. Each evening he'd reflect on his code and the day's events while writing in his personal journal. Going down his list of virtues, he revisited his day from the standpoint of each one. He'd put a check next to the virtues he'd displayed and leave a blank next to those he'd failed to practice. Amazingly, it took Franklin forty years before he actually had a day where he felt he'd been completely true to his code. That one day, he said, marked his greatest victory.

Clearly, Franklin—author, inventor, statesman—was as successful as he was because he held himself to a higher standard than anyone else could ever expect.

THE THIRTEEN VIRTUES BY WHICH BEN FRANKLIN LIVED

1.	Temperance	8.	Justice
2.	Silence	9.	Moderation
3.	Order	10.	Cleanliness
4.	Resolution	11.	Tranquillity
5.	Frugality	12.	Chastity
6.	Industry	13.	Humility
7.	Sincerity		

Now I'd like you to design your own personal code of conduct. *Think of your code as your own private compass, a way of maintaining your course even when the weather gets rough.* To start things off, I'll share my code with you as an example:

BE:

Passionate	Unique
Warm	Radiant
Silly	Healthy
Confident	Me
Happy	Emotional
Giving	Creative
Honest/genuine	Wealthy, always!

In writing down your code there is only one rule, and it's simple:

RULE: Each entry must be totally in your individual control and must be something you can "be." (It should be something you want to be on a daily basis, regardless of what happens around you.) On a sheet of paper, take some time to construct your list of personal-code values. Note: some of the values can be ones you defined earlier as important.

Now that you're done, how does it feel to have a set of standards and principles that you've decided to constantly live by? How will it affect your confidence and your attitude to know that you can win, by your own rules, every day? How much more effective will you be now that you can *feel* successful just about every day, simply by living by your own high standards?

One of Anthony Robbins's most valuable lessons is that an individual can be so much more effective by "happily achieving" instead of "achieving to be happy." That seems like just a play on words, but the fact is, *it's much more effective, and profitable, to feel good every day instead of living for a few minutes of satisfaction or recognition. You'll achieve more and enjoy it more.* That's how you win. You continually live by your code, and each day you have at least one success to carry with you to bed at night. And those successes build on one another, changing the way other people look at you as well as the way you look at yourself.

Think about this: If every day you lived by your code and made it a point to *be* everything on your list, wouldn't success follow? Wouldn't you feel so much more positive and alive if you constantly measured yourself by the things that you had total control over, instead of the things you didn't? Wouldn't that self-confidence help you find a way to increase your performance and income?

You know the answers to these questions. You would feel good continually, and that's really what we all want.

You should think of your code as a tool for self-inventory. To grow financially, or in any area, we must continually look for ways to improve on the results we're already getting. But the only way to know whether we're improving is to take stock. Determining on a daily basis whether we're adhering to our code lets us know we're on track and going forward, even if no one else has noticed yet.

As a final step in the process of becoming lifework-centered, I'm going to ask you now to complete fully a lifework matrix (listing values, purpose, lifework, and code), drawing on the work you've already done in this chapter. (A blank form is on page 92. My personal form appears opposite as an example.) Please come up with one inspiring quote that you find particularly motivating or empowering, and copy it in the space provided. Finally, keep the whole form in your planner or framed on your desk or wall, and review it every single day with the intent of committing it to memory. I actually have several copies of mine—one on my office wall, one on the wall in the study at home, one in my daily planner. Even though I've long since committed these principles to memory, I never want to get too far away from my center.

By keeping this information close to you, you make these character-building blocks a part of who you are, like all of your other experiences, knowledge, and references. You want them to become ingrained, unshakable beliefs that tell a story about the depth and quality of your spirit. To achieve wealth and greatness in your own thoughtfully designed way, you can't just learn more and do more. *You must become more.*

One point that I think can't be made enough is that it's virtually impossible to grow in just one area of life—for example, financially. *To better your financial situation you've got to do more, become more, dream more.* You have to expand who you are as a person.

For example, you've undoubtedly grown from just this short reading session. And that expansion has affected you in ways that have nothing to do with things financial. If I've done my job right, what you've read has impacted you emotionally and spiritually, boosted your confidence and self-esteem, and opened up new avenues for improving your relationships with other people. Already, you're thinking about discarding some of your previous approaches to life—and that's good. *Sometimes it's hanging on to those old ways that keeps us from growing.*

A few years back, a chimpanzee was the subject of some interesting psychological testing. Researchers fastened a jar of candy to one wall of a solitary room and placed the chimpanzee's food and water on the opposite side of the same room. The chimp, wanting the candy badly, reached his hand through the tiny opening in the neck of the jar and grabbed a giant handful. However, when he tried to remove

VALUES	EMPOWERING QUOTATION
Five Top Needs/Values	*Far better is it to dare mighty things, to win glorious triumphs, even though checkered by failure, than to take the ranks of those poor, miserable spirits who neither enjoy much nor suffer much because they live in the gray twilight that knows not victory nor defeat.*
1. *Health/Vitality*	
2. *Warmth/Love*	
3. *Passion*	
4. *Honesty/Integrity*	
5. *Making a Difference*	*—Theodore Roosevelt*

PURPOSE

I know that the purpose of my life is to be loving, compassionate, courageous, and fun; to move people and have tremendous impact in their lives; to enjoy myself and graciously accept total abundance in every area of my life. In short, to live boldly "in the zone."

LIFEWORK

To help others reach their financial dreams and improve the quality of their lives!

CODE

BE:	
Passionate	*Giving*
Warm	*Honest*
Silly	*Unique*
Confident	*Healthy*
Happy	*Creative*
	Wealthy, always!

VALUES	EMPOWERING QOUTATION

Five Top Needs/Values

1.

2.

3.

4.

5.

PURPOSE

LIFEWORK

CODE

the candy, he found that his hand—spread open and bulging—was too large for the opening. He found himself with one hand caught in the candy jar, while his food and water was entirely out of reach.

The obvious solution was to let go of at least some of the candy so the smaller fist could safely exit the candy jar. In that way the chimp could take a little at a time until he had all the candy, *and* have his food and water too. But the chimp was too frustrated to back off and view the problem from a different perspective. He was committed to his course of action because that's the way it had always happened in the past. If he wanted something, he just walked right up and took it. Eventually the chimp began banging his head against the wall, and the researchers released him, convinced that he would starve to death before he let go of his handful of candy. Alas, if only he had *let go*, he could have attained all that he desired.

Like that chimpanzee, human beings sometimes don't see the obvious solution either. Too frequently we bang our heads against the wall trying to grow the way we always have in the past. Unfortunately, personal growth doesn't work that way—we *must* expand our knowledge and our tools. If you remember only one thing from this chapter, remember this: *The same level of thinking that got you where you are, no matter how successful you may be, is not the same level of thinking that will take you where you want to go.*

Having said that, I ask you to take a step back—from your present level of thinking—and ask yourself whether seeking your dream, the way I've described, is worth trying. Are your dreams worth the uneasiness required to let go of the chains that have held you in the past? You can always go back to your old ways, but if it makes sense for you, let go and give it an honest effort. I know you'll see significant results.

PART 3

PASSIVE WEALTH CREATION

WEALTH RITUAL 3

Maintain a Plan— the Map Becomes the Territory

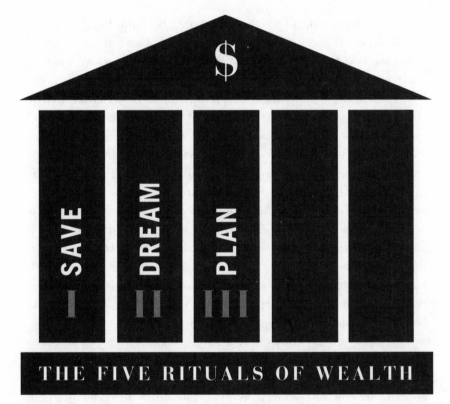

SAVE I

DREAM II

PLAN III

THE FIVE RITUALS OF WEALTH

> ## Make no little plans;
> ## they have no magic to stir men's blood. . . .
> ## Make big plans; aim high in hope and work,
> ## remembering that a noble, logical diagram
> ## once recorded will never die.
>
> —DANIEL HUDSON BURNHAM,
> ARCHITECT

TO THOSE WHO FREQUENT IT IN THE 1920s, Palm Beach seems a heaven on earth. Situated on the northern end of an eighteen-square-mile island off the southeast coast of Florida, it is America's wealthiest resort community—a winter playground for the rich and famous. Drinking in the lush affluence that surrounds him, William Gray Warden feels he has arrived. At the tip of the island, in the middle of the most beautiful landscape imaginable, stands his newly built two-story mansion—his dream. It has everything: breathtaking views, magnificent gardens, and comfortable, spacious living quarters. The first story is elegant and perfectly suited for entertaining. The second story is ideal for living and working. No doubt about it, his home is aesthetically perfect. It has class. It has cachet. The only trouble is, it has no stairway! Warden is perplexed. How is he to travel between the first and second floors? In disbelief, he asks Mizner, the architect, for a copy of the blueprints so he can figure out why his house has no stairs. Caught off-guard, the architect quickly replies: "Why, the house isn't done yet. Construction first, blueprints afterward."

Almost everyone knows that to succeed in any area you've got to have a plan. We're so familiar with this concept that sometimes we take it for granted and forget to practice the fundamentals that got us where we are in the first place. The fact is, you've got to *constantly* maintain a plan if you ever want to reach your goal. Just as you can't exercise once and expect to be fit for life, in your financial life you must constantly know where you are, where you're going, and how you're going to get there.

So many people make the mistake of planning their finances once and thinking they can relax, since they trudged through the process and lived. Or worse, they never even take the time to develop that first plan and implement it. We know the statistics: Most people spend more time planning a two-week vacation than they do planning their whole lives, and less on planning their finances. It's astonishing to learn that 95 percent of self-proclaimed financial failures feel they could have been successful if only they had had a plan. If you wish to reach your destination, it's essential that you plan *now*.

PLANNING: THE CRUCIAL FACTOR

You may be familiar with the Harvard University study on goal setting and planning that was done back in the 1950s. The graduating class of 1953 was interviewed, and each person was asked whether they had a clear, specific set of goals written down with a plan for achieving them. Only 3 percent had written goals and plans outlining exactly what they wanted for their future. Twenty years later, in 1973, the researchers went back and interviewed the members of the class of 1953. They discovered that the 3 percent with written goals were worth more, in financial terms, than the other 97 percent combined! They also seemed to be happier, healthier, and more successful than their non-goal-setting counterparts.

Think about that. We're not just talking about a modest difference in wealth. We're talking about a massive difference in lifestyles. The top 3 percent eclipsed the other 97 percent put together, despite the fact that they all shared one of the best educations money can buy. Goal setting is powerful stuff.

Most people I talk to believe that setting goals and monitoring progress toward their fulfillment really works, yet they choose not to do it. Perhaps they tried it once and it didn't work immediately. That may be because they weren't really committed to achieving their goal, they just *wished*. Some people also tell me they've set and achieved goals in the past and know it works but don't have any goals right now. I've never understood how that can be, since we all need some reason to get up in the morning—something to shoot for. I suspect these people really do have goals but can't see them with sufficient clarity, so they haven't mapped out a plan to attain them.

I set goals about twice a year, and it works great. Every time I sit down to do it, I think it's overkill and possibly a waste of time—after all, I did it just six months ago. But as soon as I get out my goal notebook, I realize my life has changed so much that a lot of my goals and plans are no longer valid. It's a good idea to get yourself a notebook and keep all of your financial goals and plans in it.

The first step is to find out where you want to be—what you want your finances to look like. I hear people say, "I just want financial independence." That's fine, but as a goal that's not sufficiently specific and precise. If you want financial independence, you can have it right now. Just quit your job and join a nomadic tribe like the Australian aborigines. You won't need a nickel.

What most people mean by financial independence is freedom from money worries *plus* the ability to maintain a certain standard of living without any effort. That's impossible, of course. The only way to get rid of money worries is to not have any—money, that is. True, you can minimize worry with proper planning and effort, but to want wealth without *any* responsibility is not a goal, it's a fairy tale. It was pointed out earlier in the book that none of us can have everything we want—we all have to make choices. That's where goal setting and financial planning come into play. We have to decide what we want—college for our kids? A new car? A retirement home in Florida?—and set a plan into action to achieve the desired result.

In setting financial goals, most people place the greatest emphasis on their retirement. After getting that gold watch, they want to maintain their standard of living and have the opportunity to do the things they love to do such as travel, visit family, or play golf. Some people never want to retire, and their goals include mansions, yachts, and owning small countries. Whatever your goal is, just remember: It won't happen by itself. There has to be a plan. To achieve your dreams you must practice Wealth Ritual 3: **Maintain a plan; the map becomes the territory.**

TWO BROTHERS

Thanks to the power of compound interest, saving for your future early in life is always better than starting later. To illustrate, let's look at two twin brothers, Billy-Bob and Joe-Bob. Billy-Bob begins saving at age twenty-one. He decides to put $2,000 a year into an IRA (individual retirement account). He does this for ten years (until he's thirty) and never saves another nickel. Meanwhile, his brother Joe-Bob saves nothing for ten years but invests $2,000 a year in his IRA for the next twenty years (from age thirty-one to fifty). Who is better off? The brother who started early but invested half as much, or the brother who started late?

As you can see from the table on the next page, Billy-Bob, who started saving earlier, is far better off than Joe-Bob, who waited ten years to begin thinking about his future. In fact, Billy-Bob's portfolio is 50 percent larger than his brother's and was substantially less painful to accumulate because he only needed to save half the amount to reach his goal. Even when inflation is considered, he quadrupled his brother's investment return because he chose not to procrastinate and decided to let time work for him. The lesson is clear: Don't underestimate the power of starting early and the effect of compound interest in helping to make your financial dreams come true.

I should point out that neither the table we just looked at nor the ones we'll be seeing shortly factor in a value for inflation. Straight calculations of compound interest will give you a future numerical value, but they can't tell you what that money will buy in the future. There's simply no easy way to predict the price of bread, milk, or housing over the next ten years. A good rule of thumb is to subtract roughly 5 percent from your annual returns and chalk it up to inflation. For example, if you're expecting to achieve 15 percent in annual returns, use the 10 percent figure so you can have a more accurate idea of the future purchasing power of your savings.

THE TIME OF YOUR LIFE

I've heard it said that there are three financial periods in life: the learning period, the earning period, and the yearning—or golden—period. The first covers the years of formal education when you're dependent on someone else, while the second covers the years spent chasing the almighty dollar, hoping your future will be a golden period, *not* a yearning period. I've always found this depiction of life's "financial timeline" to be self-defeating.

TWO BROTHERS

Each invests $2,000 a year for different periods of time. Beginning early has tremendous benefits!

AGE	BILLY-BOB	JOE-BOB
21	$2,000	
22	2,000	
23	2,000	
24	2,000	
25	2,000	
26	2,000	
27	2,000	
28	2,000	
29	2,000	
30	2,000	
31		2,000
32		2,000
33		2,000
34		2,000
35		2,000
36		2,000
37		2,000
38		2,000
39		2,000
40		2,000
41		2,000
42		2,000
43		2,000
44		2,000
45		2,000
46		2,000
47		2,000
48		2,000
49		2,000
50		2,000
Total Invested	$20,000	$40,000
TOTAL VALUE ASSUME 8%	$145,841	$98,846

As we've discussed, there's too much emphasis placed on breaking our backs in the learning and earning periods so we can be happy in our "golden" years. Your learning and earning years should be equally happy, if not more so, because you're contributing to the world in a constructive way. Also, most of the best memories of life—meeting the person of your dreams, children, career victories, family, your first home—occur during the learning and earning periods. So be wary of adopting a means-to-an-end mentality. Enduring painful sacrifice for most of your life in order to enjoy a few "golden" years doesn't make much sense.

I have developed my own version of life's three financial periods (or journeys, if you will). They are: the **learning journey,** the **earning journey,** and the **serving journey.**

There are always going to be periods in which our priorities and concerns differ and one specific financial focus dominates. Even so, the successful people I've met find a way to learn, earn, and serve on a daily basis. Let's take a look at each of these important—and, ideally, overlapping—journeys.

THE LEARNING JOURNEY

For many of us, the earliest financial period of life is dominated by formal education. During this period we tend to be dependent on others for our basic necessities. We lack financial resources, but we do our best to convince ourselves that the situation is only temporary. Often we worry that the "real world" won't greet us with open arms—that no one will offer us a job. Fear can be a large part of our mind-set. However, for the most part, we remain optimistic that our finances will improve.

THE EARNING JOURNEY

This is the period when most people focus on their careers and put everything else on the back burner. It's a race! Who can get more, do more, be more? He who dies with the most toys wins! It lasts thirty to forty years, and once again that familiar emotion, fear, manifests itself. We're scared to death we might fall behind. We're frightened that we might not have enough money to send our kids to college or buy them braces. We want to save for retirement, but there just isn't enough to go around. Perhaps we can put in more hours or get a better-paying job. This period is where most people give up their lives in the pursuit of "making a living." Some continue to grow, learn, earn, and love what they do. However, it's a reality of life that many work only for the paycheck.

The closer people get to retirement, the more frightened they become. They begin saving in record amounts, sacrificing today for tomorrow's security. Most people make the mistake of believing that they will really save big-time when their earnings increase. This rarely happens. The key is not to wait and try to scoop huge savings from a colossal income. Rather, you need to save small amounts from the modest income you'll begin receiving once you enter the working world. Believe me, there's a lot of money passing through your hands. Take a look at the following table to get an idea of just how much:

HOW MUCH MONEY WILL PASS THROUGH YOUR HANDS?

MONTHLY INCOME	10 YEARS	20 YEARS	30 YEARS	40 YEARS
$1,000	$120,000	$240,000	$360,000	$480,000
1,500	180,000	360,000	540,000	720,000
2,000	240,000	480,000	720,000	960,000
2,500	300,000	600,000	900,000	1,200,000
3,000	360,000	720,000	1,080,000	1,440,000
3,500	420,000	840,000	1,260,000	1,680,000
4,000	480,000	960,000	1,440,000	1,920,000
4,500	540,000	1,080,000	1,620,000	2,160,000
5,000	600,000	1,200,000	1,800,000	2,400,000

THE SERVING JOURNEY

I look at the final period of our financial lives as being characterized chiefly by service. You either serve yourself by doing exactly what you've deprived yourself of for years, or you serve other people, using your time to make an even greater contribution than you have in the past. Unfortunately, most people never get to experience this hearty portion of life. Instead, they live in financial lack, still fraught with worry. All they can think about is surviving.

Even retirees who have a solid financial foundation under them experience fear. In fact, sometimes it's that fear that gets them off their duffs. They become afraid that they might regret not giving more, not making more of a difference. That's why you see many of them running for public office, writing their first novel, or working with the homeless. The "retired life" can be truly exhilarating if your financial worries are out of the way. Financial abundance won't just happen, however; it takes planning. Make a commitment to do whatever it takes to become the best person you can be. It all begins with taking care of your own security first.

How much money will you need when you retire? Many experts suggest that 60 to 80 percent of your working income should be sufficient. However, if you plan a major lifestyle change, such as a lot of traveling, you'll probably need more. Also, you'll need to account for inflation. Your income must be constantly increasing because prices are. For example: If you need $80,000 your first year in retirement and inflation averages 6 percent, you'll need $143,200 to support the same lifestyle in ten years and $256,000 in twenty years!

OUR PROBLEM/OPPORTUNITY

Today, as I write, a man who is sixty-five years of age can expect to live to be eighty-two. A woman, age sixty-five, can expect to live to be eighty-six. Medical science is keeping us alive longer, and I think that's great. Especially when you consider that the average life expectancy in 1900 was age forty-seven. I hope we can continue to achieve the same life-lengthening results in the next decade. Maybe we can look forward to being ninety, one hundred, or more.

Think about that for a minute, though. You could spend more time retired than you did working! The assets you accumulate in your working life have to support you in the twenty, thirty, or forty years after retirement (assuming you won't be able to rely on Social Security, and these days that seems a pretty fair assumption).

The fact is, there are many retirees today who are outliving their money. To fully appreciate the gravity of the problem, consider that a retirement income of $2,000 a month—which was a good income fifteen years ago—is worth about $800 in today's dollars. The implication of this is that even those who planned well are facing extreme difficulty. They saved some, but either they didn't save enough or they didn't put their savings where it could really work for them.

The excuse for not saving that I get from people in their forties, fifties, sixties, and even older is that "it's too late." These people feel discouraged because they believe there's not enough time left to build the wealth they desire. That's absolutely false! Most of us are just beginning the second half of our life when we cross the middle-age mark, but we've been conditioned to think that our prime, productive working years are winding down. Most likely, we're all going to live longer than our parents did, but that's okay, because we're entering a new age, the information age, a time where youth doesn't matter as much. Most of our professions no longer require young, strong bodies to perform physical labor. Feeling like you're too old to make your dreams happen just doesn't make sense.

You should view all of the years of experience you've accumulated as preparation for the truly hearty time of your life. This could be a time to discover your other talents and lifework, instead of relying on the skills of youth that defined your past. A few years ago I attended a lecture given by Og Mandino, the noted self-help author. He was probably seventy-five years old at the time, but his performance and delivery were better than ever. All his years of experience gave him an edge, but I wouldn't have experienced the value of hearing him speak if he'd accepted traditional ideas of age, wealth, and work.

Remember how age became an issue when Ronald Reagan ran for president in 1980? During his campaign he redefined our ideas of age when his younger opponent made a reference to his being too old to perform his presidential duties effectively. The over-sixty crowd cheered when he humorously stated that he "had no intention of making an issue of my opponent's youth and inexperience." Reagan went on to serve two terms as the oldest president in history, and to this day is still active on the lecture circuit.

At one of my recent speaking engagements I met a retired doctor in his seventies who'd used

> **First, have a definite, clear, practical ideal—a goal, an objective. Second, have the necessary means to achieve your ends—wisdom, money, materials, and methods. Third, adjust all your means to that end.**
>
> **—ARISTOTLE**

his time away from work to write a fitness book for "middle-aged muscles." He was proud of his accomplishment, as well he should be. The information he imparted in his book has the potential to affect readers for years to come. But the point is, he would never have attempted a project of this magnitude if he'd felt he was "over the hill." In fact, his experience and age opened a new door for him, one that wouldn't have been there twenty years earlier.

We've also heard the story of Colonel Sanders, of Kentucky Fried Chicken fame. He didn't even begin to build his franchise until he was sixty-five and had received his first, measly Social Security check. This man didn't leave his mark until after the world considered him past his prime. Indeed, from a marketing perspective, his "persona" wouldn't have been as effective if he'd been thirty years younger. His age and grandfatherly image actually helped make him successful.

The point of these examples is this: *Active* and *passive* wealth creation do take time. But advancements in health and medical care have made traditional notions of life span passé. It turns out that we have an extended period in which to save, invest, and make a difference, and it's incumbent on all of us to take advantage of it.

Ironically, I often hear people in their twenties and thirties say they're "too young" to think about financial planning. To young, too old—when *is* a good time? I say *now!* Regardless of your age or youth, now is the time to begin planning. And if you don't see a way to save enough, look into a second career when you retire. It could be the most successful and rewarding adventure of your life.

If I have one message for people on the verge of retirement, it's this: *It's never too late to make your financial dreams a reality, but there'll always be an excuse not to do so.* Since we're living longer, our "working" years can't be spent frivolously, especially if we're nearing retirement. We have to make each and every year count by saving what we can and constantly following a financial plan. No one else is going to do it for us.

Let me share with you an exercise I've developed to emphasize the urgency of beginning to save and plan today. Please take five seconds to complete it. I think it will be an eye-opener.

ON THE TIMELINE BELOW:

1. Mark your current age with an *X*.
2. Mark the age at which you want to retire with an *X* (if you don't know, use age sixty-five).
3. Now shade everything from the left of your age—all the way to zero.
4. Now shade everything from the right of your proposed retirement age—all the way to one hundred (or stop at eighty-five if you're a pessimist and think you'll just live to meet the averages).

```
┌──────────────────────────────────────────────────────────┐
│                                                            │
└──────────────────────────────────────────────────────────┘
```
0 5 10 15 20 25 30 35 40 45 50 55 60 65 70 75 80 85 90 95 100

The time shaded to the left is gone. The time on the right will be spent in retirement. *The area in the middle represents the time you have left to best save for and design your happy, secure future!*

If you're up in years, you may be discouraged—but don't be. In the next few sections you'll learn exactly how to maximize your time and achieve all of your financial goals.

GOAL SETTING

To achieve anything in life we have to decide what we really want and then choose which goals are most important to us and should be achieved first. The following fill-in chart is designed to help you get a clear picture of what's most important to you right now. Rank the listed goals in order of their importance to you, and put a time horizon on each—that is, specify when you'd like to have each accomplished. Next, choose one or two of the goals that you'd like to go to work on immediately, and write down steps you can take right away to help you achieve them. We'll discuss each goal category in the following pages.

FINANCIAL GOALS

RANK	GOAL	TIME HORIZON
_____	Retire comfortably	_____
_____	Buy a home	_____
_____	Children's education	_____
_____	Build investment portfolio	_____
_____	Tax-free income	_____

What can I do right away to begin achieving my most important goals?

_____

_____

_____

_____

_____

(Hint: Finishing this book would be a good start!)

GOAL: RETIRING COMFORTABLY

The biggest financial concern people have is retirement. They want to be able to enjoy the same standard of living after they no longer get a regular paycheck. This can be done relatively easily if a proper plan is developed, followed, and given enough time to create sufficient wealth to support you. Right now, though, there are over 75 million Americans who aren't saving enough for retirement. These people will either change their ways or become financial statistics. Let's take a brief personal inventory to see how you compare.

How much should you have saved by now? The table below provides amounts needed *in addition to* a pension.

Do you like what the table is telling you? I'm always reluctant to compare people with the averages. Who wants to be average? No one, I hope! You should use the chart as a comparison, not as a goal. Set your own goals. You alone decide where you'll end up.

When you're setting goals and planning for retirement, think about the following questions and discuss them with your financial

HOW MUCH SHOULD YOU HAVE SAVED BY NOW?

If you are:	And your age is:			
A married couple	**35**	**45**	**55**	**65**
earning $75,000	$11,450	$75,090	$229,890	$367,800
earning 100,000	36,120	118,400	287,710	520,810
earning 150,000	67,930	199,760	503,930	891,700
A single man				
earning $50,000	$6,330	$36,110	$95,700	$172,210
earning 75,000	10,250	89,470	253,400	370,930
earning 100,000	28,600	129,000	299,240	511,000
A single woman				
earning $50,000	$35,650	$72,850	$126,800	$189,960
earning 75,000	61,220	149,350	259,600	361,370
earning 100,000	89,560	203,340	361,110	539,460

SOURCE: Merrill Lynch Baby-Boom Retirement Index, as seen in *Time* magazine. Figures are in 1991 dollars needed in addition to a pension. Without a pension, you'll need to save much more.

consultant, if you have one (don't worry if your numbers are estimates; you can change them over time):

RETIREMENT PLANNING QUESTIONS TO ASK YOURSELF

- When do I plan to retire?
- How much income will I need at retirement?
- What sources of income do I expect to have?
- How much, in personal assets, will I need to
  accumulate?
- How much can I save each year or month?

I've observed that most people struggle in trying to estimate their
retirement needs and sources of income. The next few pages discuss
different income sources people can draw from when retirement day
finally arrives. In order, they are:

1. Social Security
2. Your company retirement plan
3. Your personal retirement plan
4. Your savings

SOCIAL SECURITY

The income you'll receive from your Social Security benefits is
based on how much you've earned, how long you've worked, and
when you'll retire. You can call the Social Security Administration
(1-800-772-1213, ask for form SSA-7004) and get an estimate of
the benefits you'll receive based upon your projected retirement date.
Factoring in inflation, you'll see that the annual total is quite mini-
mal (hence, the need for other sources of income).

The table below represents the maximum amount you can expect
to receive from Social Security annually if you retire at age sixty-five
in the years indicated.

MAXIMUM BENEFITS, SOCIAL SECURITY

1990	$10,747
1995	$11,384
2000	$12,663

SOURCE: Shearson Lehman Brothers

One final note on Social Security. I know that we all work hard and contribute to this "fund," so it makes sense to think of the money as "guaranteed"—to assume there's no way it can be taken away. However, with the population aging so rapidly and the current complaints about the health of the Social Security system, I wouldn't want to rely too heavily on the federal government to take care of me in my golden years. I doubt the system will exist, at least in its present form, in twenty years. Since in a few short decades there'll be more older people in this country than younger people, it's probably not wise to put all your eggs in the Social Security basket. The greatest single source of income for retired people today is personal savings. This will continue to be the case—indeed, even to a larger extent—as the 75 million baby boomers begin to retire in the next twenty years. As you can see from the graph below, most of your retirement income is likely to depend on you.

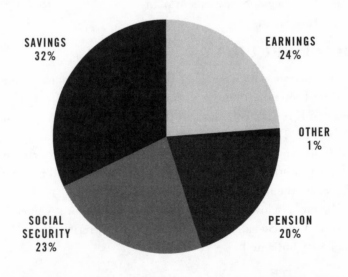

SAVINGS
32%

EARNINGS
24%

OTHER
1%

PENSION
20%

SOCIAL
SECURITY
23%

1988 SOCIAL SECURITY ESTIMATES OF INCOME SOURCES DURING RETIREMENT

For retirees 65 and older living on $20,000 or more per year

SOURCE: Social Security Administration

YOUR COMPANY RETIREMENT PLAN

If you're fortunate enough to work for a company with a qualified plan to help you save, use it! This is one of the best ways to save for your future. This plan might be called a 401(k) if you work for a corporation, a 403(b) if you work for a nonprofit organization, or a Keogh plan if you're self-employed (or work for a sole proprietorship or partnership). With these types of plans you can elect to have money deducted straight from your paycheck—before taxes and before you ever see it. This is the easiest and most beneficial way to save because not only do you get the tax advantage, you're also "forced" into saving every single payday.

Most plans direct your investments into different types of mutual funds according to risk and return. I usually advise individuals to contribute the maximum to their company-sponsored plans (usually up to 15 percent of earned income) before opening any other type of investment account. It makes sense to invest *before* taxes first. The drawback of company plans is that you're penalized in most cases for early withdrawal (before age fifty-nine and a half). In some cases, you can withdraw your money early, without penalties except the taxes due, for emergency (see IRS definitions) or as a down payment on your primary residence. Ask your employer for a detailed description of your plan, and find out about your eligibility to participate.

If your company doesn't have a retirement plan or you aren't eligible, you can contribute to an IRA. No matter what your situation, there's a way to save some money on a tax-deductible (or before-tax) basis. If you need help, seek a financial advisor.

YOUR PERSONAL RETIREMENT PLAN

In America, a personal retirement plan usually means an IRA. An individual retirement account is set up specifically for your retirement savings and investments. In an IRA your investment return compounds tax-deferred until you make a withdrawal. If you qualify, your contributions to the plan may also be tax-deductible. If you have an employer-sponsored retirement plan, you may not qualify for a tax deduction; however, your money still grows on a tax-deferred basis until you take it out. Uncle Sam wants you to save for your

> **A goal is a dream with a deadline.**
>
> —STEVE SMITH,
> AMDAHL
> CORPORATION

retirement, and there are tremendous tax benefits to doing so. Here's the bottom line: *If you aren't contributing to a company-sponsored retirement plan, open an IRA.* You can contribute up to $2,000 a year and deduct it from your income when it comes tax time—it's a beautiful thing. If you have a company-sponsored retirement plan, you may still qualify for a partial deduction (see an accountant or financial advisor to learn more about this). Either way, deductible or not, your account grows tax-deferred. No taxes on gains and interest are due until you withdraw the money at retirement.

Make sure you understand the laws before you open an account. There *are* catches. For example, if you withdraw your money before age fifty-nine and a half, you'll incur a 10 percent penalty in addition to the taxes. However, there's a way around the penalty by withdrawing your money in substantially equal payments and special "financial hardship" cases as determined by the IRS. If you have questions, most brokerage firms, banks, or accounting firms have brochures that explain the rules.

I won't bother here to give you the IRS code on IRAs for two reasons: first, it's boring (if you truly need the code, you probably already have it), and second, it may change soon. Here are some general guidelines to help you determine whether or not your contribution is deductible:

If neither you nor your spouse is an active participant in an employer-sponsored retirement plan:

A full deduction for each of you (up to $2,000) is still allowed regardless of your modified adjusted gross income or tax-filing status (assuming that you don't contribute more than you earn that year).

If either you or your spouse is an active participant in an employer-sponsored retirement plan:

A full or partial deduction for each of you may still be allowed, depending on your modified adjusted gross income and your tax-filing status. Exhibit 3 (in the back of this book) discusses the partial deduction you may qualify for.

No deduction will be allowed if your modified adjusted gross income is above the following levels:

$35,000 for a single filer

$50,000 combined for married individuals filing jointly

$10,000 for each spouse, when married individuals file separately and either is covered by an employer-sponsored plan

Contributing consistently to an IRA is an incredible tool if used properly. When I talk about IRAs at my seminars I'm continually amazed at how many people don't really understand them fully. A lot of people think an IRA is an investment. It's *not* an investment. It is merely an account that can hold investments. This misunderstanding is due largely to bank advertising. Most banks post their "IRA rates" in the window. What they are really saying is that the investment inside your IRA is paying a certain percentage return. The investment is usually a CD or a money-market fund. Your IRA money can be invested in many types of vehicles, including CDs, stocks, bonds, and mutual funds. You should think of an IRA as an umbrella—a shell, an account. Many different investments and types of investments can be inside the account.

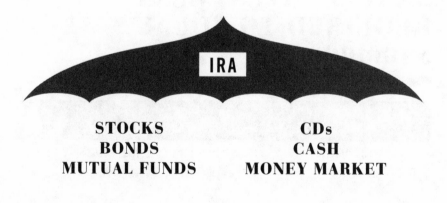

STOCKS   **CDs**
BONDS   **CASH**
MUTUAL FUNDS   **MONEY MARKET**

YOUR SAVINGS

It goes without saying that the more savings you have, the more secure you'll feel. Because some tax-advantaged retirement plans put caps on how much you can contribute annually, and because the money steered into these plans can't easily be accessed in the short term, you'll need to save in an outside account as well. If you don't trust yourself to make regular contributions, be aware that most brokerage firms and mutual funds have automatic investment programs that make monthly deductions from your checking or savings account. It's a great, easy way to save consistently and fits hand in glove with an investment principle I'll explain later called dollar cost averaging.

The best way to decide how much you're willing to save and invest on a consistent basis is to work backward. That is, decide how much you'll need at retirement, make some assumptions about your investment returns, and calculate how much you'll need to save on a yearly or monthly basis. The chart below should give you an idea of what it will take to realize your dreams.

As you can see, the power of compound interest is mind-boggling. If you have thirty years until retirement and can average a 15 percent return, you can reach your $100,000 goal by saving only $230 a year, or $414 per year at 12 percent! If you want an approxi-

APPROXIMATE ANNUAL INVESTMENT REQUIRED TO EQUAL $100,000

	5 YEARS	10 YEARS	15 YEARS	20 YEARS	25 YEARS	30 YEARS	35 YEARS	40 YEARS
3%	$18,836	8,723	5,377	3,722	2,743	2,102	1,654	1,326
6%	17,740	7,587	4,296	2,718	1,823	1,265	897	646
9%	16,709	6,582	3,406	1,955	1,181	734	464	296
12%	15,741	5,698	2,682	1,388	750	414	232	130
15%	14,832	4,925	2,102	976	470	230	114	56
18%	13,978	4,252	1,640	682	292	126	55	24

mation of a monthly savings amount, just divide by twelve. If your goal is $1 million, just multiply your yearly contribution by ten. (The reason this multiplication works is

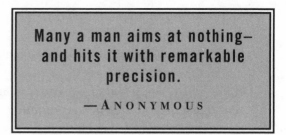

that you are multiplying the two factors—annual investment and goal—by the same number, while leaving the percentage and duration the same.)

There is a compound-interest table in the back of this book (Exhibit 4) for your convenience, but remember, we're using numerical values only. You'll want to figure in an inflation factor of, say, 5 percent to get a rough idea of your future purchasing power. To do this, just drop your expected return by your inflation factor, from, say, 15 percent to 10 percent. Manipulate the data any way you see fit, then set your goals and take action toward their completion.

GOAL: BUYING A HOME

Owning your own home can be one of life's most pleasurable and rewarding experiences—it's part of nearly everyone's dream. It can also be very expensive. A home purchase is the largest investment and the largest commitment most families ever make. When you settle into the community of your choice, you gain a stake in its future plans and problems. Most people feel a sense of responsibility and pride in their neighborhoods. Consequently, owning a home is much more than a financial decision. What house you choose will determine who you'll live near and what school your kids will go to and will influence how you're perceived among your peers.

Financially speaking, it seems that everyone wants you to own a home. The government encourages you by making the interest on your mortgage tax-deductible. Virtually everyone you do business with asks you on the new-account application whether you rent or own, as if to suggest home ownership makes one more financially responsible. The prevailing attitude seems to be that unless you own, you're still in a nomadic state, liable to skip town and leave your creditors in the dust.

In my opinion, owning your own home is the best investment you can make, because it forces you to save and build equity in something. Most people won't stick to a monthly investment plan, but they'll pay their mortgage every month without fail. The fear of being thrown out into the street forces them to stick to their mortgage. And, if they're lucky, they should be able to look up after thirty years and find they've accumulated substantial net worth because of their home's appreciation.

Of course, part of the reason for the boom in housing prices that characterized the 1970s and 1980s was the demand generated by first-time baby boomer home buyers. As we pass though the 1990s, demand has softened, making it less likely that homeowners will make a killing by selling in the next ten years. Still, homes rarely depreciate over the long term, and since these things tend to run in cycles, there's always the chance that you'll catch the wave.

It's true that for some people owning a home is not the best idea. For them it makes more sense to use the money they'll tie up in lawn care, painting, and plumbing bills to build a business or invest for their future. Depending on their situation, leasing a home may be an attractive option. The important thing to remember is that even if buying doesn't seem like the best use of your money but you feel you want to own your house, buy it! If for you the feelings of security, achievement, commitment, or responsibility are attached to owning a home—and you don't mind the maintenance costs—then by all means go for it.

If you intend to buy a home soon, you need to save for your down payment. Speak to a mortgage lender to get an idea of what you can afford and how much of a down payment you'll need. The cash needed to close on the average American home last year was around $28,000 (source: Merrill Lynch). If you save $500 a month and get a 12 percent return, you should have the down payment in about four years. Keep in mind: *The price of the home you buy should not exceed two times your family income, and you shouldn't pay more than 38 percent of income (after federal income tax) for your monthly housing expenses (mortgage, taxes, utilities, maintenance, etc.).*

GOAL: FUNDING CHILDREN'S EDUCATION

One of the most valuable gifts you can give your children is the opportunity for a good college education. Unfortunately, most parents these days aren't able to foot the bill themselves. In some cases grandparents are being called on to help out. With proper planning you can help your children or grandchildren in this financially difficult time. Costs are going up dramatically, so getting started right away is a must.

As you can see from the above table, higher education is very expensive. However, a college degree will undoubtedly pay off. Increased earnings over your child's lifetime is just one of the rewards of earning a degree. Median household income for college graduates is more than 50 percent higher than for high school graduates. Students who go on to earn advanced degrees are even better off financially.

AVERAGE ANNUAL COLLEGE COSTS

Academic Year	Four-Year Public	Four-Year Private
1975	$2,650	$4,205
1980	3,380	6,060
1985	5,314	9,659
1990	6,671	14,326
1995	9,357	20,094
2000	13,124	28,183
2005	18,405	39,528
2010	25,817	55,440

Includes tuition, room and board, fees, etc.
SOURCE: 1975–1990, The College Board; 1995–2000, projection of 7% annual increase

However, graduate schools of business, law, engineering, and medicine are extremely expensive. If you want to help your child with college, it's never too early.

Make a worksheet that states approximately what year each of your children will enter college, estimate the costs, and work backward to determine how much you'll need to save per month. If you have quite a while until your kids reach college age, you can rely, in part, on compound interest helping you out. Use the compound interest table in the back of this book or a financial calculator to find out exactly how little you can get away with saving.

GOAL: BUILDING AN INVESTMENT PORTFOLIO

We're going to discuss building an investment portfolio in detail in the next chapter; however, if you're just starting out, this needs to be a priority goal, so you have to plan for it. As I mentioned previously, a good rule of thumb is to save no less than 10 percent of every single paycheck. Make that your first priority; make it a *must*! Use your company retirement plan if you have one. After you've maxed out on your contribution to that, explore other investment alternatives. I think mutual funds are great for small investors. They're easy, convenient, and you can open one for as little as $250 to $500. Some funds will even deduct the money from your checking account every month if you wish.

I've already stressed the wisdom of investing in common stocks because it's the best way to achieve passive growth over the long term. However, if you have short-term objectives, there are other classes of securities that can be particularly useful. For example, let's say you've already built a considerable portfolio and you want to retire and sail around the world with your kids. Your objectives have changed. Growth is no longer the most important consideration; your investment priority has now shifted toward income. That's where bonds or cash fit in. If your objective is to draw every dollar of income you can from your portfolio, you might want to be 100 percent invested in bonds or other interest-bearing instruments. On the other hand, if your objective is to maximize growth, you might want to be 100 percent invested in stocks or mutual funds.

I'll discuss stock and stock mutual fund investments in greater detail in the pages to come, because the chief thrust of this book is how to *grow* your net worth. But you should understand that your objectives may shift over time, so your portfolio should be adjusted accordingly. Eventually, you may want some growth *and* some income. In that case a mix, or "balance," would be appropriate.

A good way to build a solid balanced or mixed portfolio is by diversifying your investments by asset class. For our purposes, the discussion can be confined to three classes of securities: *stocks*, *bonds*, and *cash* (safe money-market instruments).

According to economist Harry Markowitz, who won the Nobel Prize in 1990 for his work in modern portfolio theory, most of an investor's return in a given portfolio can be attributed to the *class* of security (stocks, bonds, cash) as opposed to the *individual selection* of securities. Also, he found that risk can be reduced if an individual "balances" his portfolio by diversifying among several types of investments. However, any time an investor reduces his risk, he also reduces his return over time. Because risk is such an important factor to small investors especially, most professionals recommend a portfolio blend of stocks, bonds, and cash. A good place to start is by diversifying your portfolio among asset classes in a way that makes you comfortable. If you want it all in stocks or stock funds, then do it. If you feel better with half in stocks and half in bonds, that's okay too. If you wish, you can mathematically uncover the optimum balance and most efficient asset mix. But the most important thing is to find your comfort zone, because each adjustment in your mix also changes your risk levels.

I used to try to get all of my clients to follow the analysts' asset-allocation recommendations because these experts are paid to study and make suggestions that maximize return while minimizing risk. I thought that this rational, mathematical approach would work well for investors. It did—with institutional accounts that managed money with less emotion. However, with the individual accounts I worked with it was a different story. No matter how logical the approach, people still go with their gut feelings when it comes to making money decisions. I'm not saying that's right or wrong. The point is that if everyone on Wall Street recommends being 90 percent invested in stocks but you lose sleep with that much money in the market, don't do it. I want everyone to maximize return, and to do so requires attention to asset allocation, but you have to ask yourself if it's worth it to you to go against your gut instincts or worry yourself sick by following other people's recommendations. You need to find the point at which *you* feel comfortable with your asset mix. As for me, with the exception of some emergency cash, I'm 100 percent invested in the stock market. That doesn't bother me. I have conservative stocks and aggressive stocks, and funds that are equally varying in their approach. I own no bonds because they don't fill my current financial needs.

By the way, I do recommend that you keep enough cash on hand to cover two to three months of living expenses. Cash isn't really an investment, but it does represent a safe haven for special situations and emergencies.

Here are examples of three typical middle-aged investors' portfolios:

PORTFOLIOS OF THREE INVESTORS

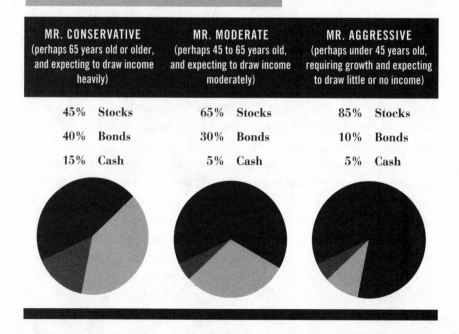

MR. CONSERVATIVE (perhaps 65 years old or older, and expecting to draw income heavily)		MR. MODERATE (perhaps 45 to 65 years old, and expecting to draw income moderately)		MR. AGGRESSIVE (perhaps under 45 years old, requiring growth and expecting to draw little or no income)	
45%	Stocks	65%	Stocks	85%	Stocks
40%	Bonds	30%	Bonds	10%	Bonds
15%	Cash	5%	Cash	5%	Cash

GOAL: TAX-FREE INCOME

In the United States May 5 is Tax Freedom Day. That's the day your accrued income for the year matches your annual tax payment. For the rest of the year, you actually get to work for yourself, not the government. On average, you work 113 days a year to pay your taxes. Taxes are a way of life, but fortunately, there are still a few ways to get an income stream free of taxation.

In the next few paragraphs we'll discuss bonds, but first let me say this: *Bonds aren't normally considered growth vehicles for individual investors.* Their value, compared with that of stocks, is relatively static. The reason people own bonds is that they throw off regular interest payments, creating a steady income stream. Hence, they fill the needs of those who have just about all of the growth they want and now need to live off the income from their investments. They also provide an extra measure of safety, since the higher-quality bond issuers promise to return all of the investor's principal after a stated time period.

Even if your priority is growth, there *is* a type of bond you should investigate because of the tax-free income it provides. I'm referring to municipal bonds. Municipals are relatively conservative and offer interest that is usually free from federal or state taxes—sometimes both. They are securities issued by state and local governments to finance public improvement projects. As a bond holder you're accepting the issuing agency's IOU to return your principal at a specified time in the future. For this, the issuer promises to pay you a stated interest rate for the life of the bond. Typically, municipal bonds are considered very safe, second only to U.S. government securities. Independent advisory services, like Moody's Investors Service and Standard & Poor's (S&P) Corporation, analyze and grade bonds according to their ability to pay back principal and interest. The single highest rating for safety is AAA (S&P) or Aaa (Moody's). In this scheme, the U.S. government rates a AAA. As the rating lowers, so does the perceived credit quality of the bond. A list of the highest bond-quality ratings (investment grade) appears on page 124.

The quality ratings continue all the way down to D (for default). Any bond rated below the range in the following list is considered "junk" and probably not the safest issue for the conservative investor.

> ## The only difference between death and taxes is that death doesn't get worse every time Congress meets.
>
> —WILL ROGERS

I've owned many bonds below this investment grade that were somewhat speculative, but I felt comfortable with the issuer.

As I've said, the holder of a bond issue normally isn't concerned with capital appreciation. At maturity, by definition, a high-quality bond can be expected to pay off your principal (usually $1,000 face value)—no more and no less. You can't get growth if the bond can only mature for the amount you have invested.

Bonds, like stocks, do trade in an active secondary market, and you can sell them above your purchase price if you have a good market—or below if the market is not so good. However, your timing has got to be right because as the bond reaches maturity, its price begins to near the principal, or face value. Trading bonds is very difficult, so I almost never recommend that people invest in bonds, or bond mutual funds, if they want their portfolio to grow. The only flirtation with the bond market they should be considering, and that's from a tax-benefit perspective only, is municipals.

←————	CREDIT QUALITY			————→
Moody's	Aaa	Aa	A	Baa
S&P	AAA	AA	A	BBB

Tax-free income, especially in this day and age, is extremely attractive. No discussion of municipal bonds would be complete without comparing tax-free returns to taxable interest: the taxable-equivalent yield. If you have a choice between a vehicle paying a taxable rate of return and a tax-free instrument, the table below will help you decide which one is best. For example, if you have a CD paying 7 percent, you're in the 28 percent tax bracket, and you're looking at a municipal bond (tax-free) that pays 5.5 percent, you're better off with the bond. This is because you'd need a taxable equivalent yield of 7.64 percent to offset the effect of taxes from the CD's earnings. Please note that we're discussing U.S. federal income taxes. If the bond is also free from local and/or state taxes, it's even more attractive. For the income-oriented investor, tax-free bonds (or a tax-free bond fund) are a wonderful tool because they provide simplicity, convenience, and safety.

Federal Tax Bracket	Tax-Free Yield						
	5%	5.5%	6%	6.5%	7%	7.5%	8%
	Taxable Equivalent Yield						
15%	5.88	6.47	7.05	7.64	8.23	8.82	9.41
28%	6.94	7.64	8.33	9.02	9.72	10.41	11.11
31%	7.25	7.97	8.70	9.42	10.14	10.87	11.59

INFLATION: THE ENEMY OF WEALTH

A newspaper reporter once asked J. Paul Getty, the American oil tycoon, if it were true that his net worth was over a billion dollars. Getty was silent for a minute or two. "I suppose so," he replied thoughtfully. "But remember, a billion dollars doesn't go as far as it used to." Beneath the humor there's a point to that story—that is, the bad guy in the money game is inflation.

Inflation—an increase in prices—has always been with us and probably always will. Consequently, as prices go up over the years, a dollar buys less and less. No matter how much money you have, unless it grows, next year it will buy less. Your purchasing power will deteriorate. The only way to keep up with inflation is to grow your assets. The only way to grow your assets is to invest it at some risk. There is no free lunch!

People ask me all the time, "Is my investment *guaranteed?*" What they're really saying is, "Will I get back the same amount of money I put in?" But is that what you want? Investing absolutely risk-free may seem, on the surface, like a smart strategy. Unfortunately, even if you keep your principal intact, next year that money will buy less, and the following years less, and less, and less. This is the most common mistake investors make. There is no guarantee in life, only opportunity. If you had $10,000 today and you took it to the bank and invested it in something "guaranteed" (maybe a CD or a money market account), in ten years what would you have? Your $10,000, plus some small interest, of course! Forget the fact that it's ten years later and your ten grand will barely take you to Disneyland. Inflation eats away at your principal every single day. *The only way to protect your assets is to put your money to work in some useful venture.*

I always hear: "But what if I invest and I lose some of it, what then?" I say you learned something. Don't be foolish, invest prudently, but do something! If you do nothing, you're guaranteed to lose what money you have over time to inflation.

I understand that some money has to be set aside for emergency or liquidity purposes. Fine. But understand that those dollars are set aside for safety and convenience, not for investment. Cash (or CDs, or money markets) is not an investment. Cash is trash when it comes to your investment returns. I also concede that there is interest paid on deposits at banks. That's what we call the "risk-free rate of return." Believe me, after inflation and taxes are factored out, *the return you realize for taking no risk is always zero!* Sometimes it's less than zero. If it sounds too good to be true, it is. There's a reason why bank buildings are almost always the biggest and nicest in town!

A quick numerical example will illustrate what I'm talking about. Suppose you put $1,000 in an insured bank CD that matures in one year. It pays 5 percent interest for the entire year.

$1,000.00 deposit
+50.00 interest at 5%

$1,050.00 total value

Not bad, right? You made $50, and your $1,000 was safe and sound, right? We'll see!

$ 1,050.00 total value
-52.50 decrease in purchasing power at 5% inflation
-15.00 taxes on $50 gain (30% bracket)

$982.50 real return considering inflation and taxes

As you can see, when you consider inflation and taxes even a reasonable return on your investment looks pretty bad. In purchasing power, you took a loss. The problem is that most people don't realize it because they still see their principal intact. This simple concept is known as "real investment return." *The real rate of return is the actual return realized after inflation is factored out.* You can double your money, but if inflation cuts its purchasing power in half, you're still even! Over the years, failure to understand this simple fact of life destroys people financially.

To fully appreciate the dilutive power of inflation, see the following price chart. It's based on a 5 percent inflation rate.

THE FUTURE IS GONNA BE EXPENSIVE!

	1993	2013
Hamburger and fries	$3.95	$10.48
Snow ski trip (for two)	$1,400.00	$3,714.62
Theater tickets (pair)	$100.00	$265.33
Compact disc	$14.95	$39.67
Mountain bike	$350.00	$928.65
Electric bill (month)	$90.00	$238.80
Pro baseball game (family)	$85.00	$225.53
New BMW (325i)	$30,000.00	$79,598.93
Home (average three-bedroom)	$120,000.00	$318,395.00

As a society, we've been taught wrong. We've been taught to hoard—to "store up" our resources, including money. But money can't be stockpiled. It's either a tool that's being used wisely or useless paper. Clearly, people have to change the way they think about risk. *True risk comes not with action but with comfortable inaction.* The only way to risk all is to do nothing. If you only arrive at one new insight from reading this book, make it this understanding of how inflation and failure to act will rob you of all wealth.

How do you neutralize the inflation monster? How do you get over your fear and begin letting your money work as hard as you do? Begin by completing and following a financial plan. Using the following Financial Planning Summary worksheet will give you a good start.

FINANCIAL PLANNING SUMMARY

Financial Goal	Amount Needed and When
Retirement	$
Children's education	
Buying a home (down payment and closing)	
Building a portfolio	

Savings Vehicle (To Reach All Financial Goals)	Monthly/Yearly Salary
Individual retirement account (IRA)	$
Spousal IRA	
Employer-sponsored plan	
Personal savings	

- Don't forget to factor in a reasonable rate of return when calculating your monthly savings rates, such as 12 or 15%.

PORTFOLIO HOLDINGS RECORD (Perhaps Top 10 Method)

	Holding	Dividend Yield	Price Paid	Price Sold	Profit/Loss
1.					
2.					
3.					
4.					
5.					
6.					
7.					
8.					
9.					
10.					

CONTRIBUTION GOALS

Cause/Organization and Why	Monthly/Yearly Contibution Goal
	$

WEALTH RITUAL 4

Employ Your Resources—
Money Goes Where It's Treated Best

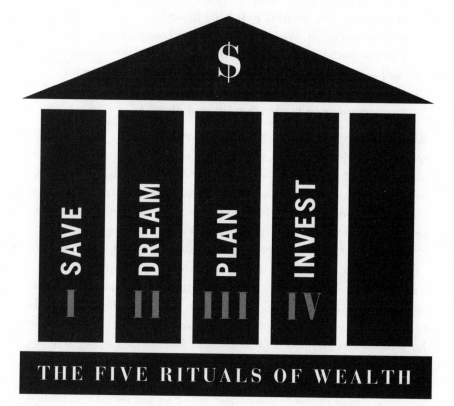

> ## There is no security in this life.
> ## There is only opportunity.
>
> —GENERAL DOUGLAS MACARTHUR

HOW I MADE MY FORTUNE
(by an unknown millionaire)

It was really quite simple. I bought an apple for five cents, spent the evening polishing it, and sold it the next day for ten cents. With this I bought two apples, spent the evening polishing them, and sold them for twenty cents. And so it went until I had amassed a few thousand dollars. It was then that I bought shares in Apple Computer Corporation and made ten million dollars.

WHAT CAN SOMETIMES BE EVEN MORE PLEASURABLE than *actively* creating wealth by using your own energy and creativity—most commonly, in the form of work—is *passively* creating wealth by investing in enterprises that are run by talented and committed people. It seems too good to be true, but the fact is that you can harness other people's abilities in the service of your own wealth creation.

Every day, the employees and management of Coca-Cola, for example, go to work and attempt to increase their company's profitability in the free market system. In the process, they also create wealth for the thousands of shareholders who own the company. In other words, Coca-Cola—and other publicly traded companies—have the ability to make us wealthy without our ever lifting a finger, making a sale, or going to a board meeting. We can passively increase our own net worth simply by owning shares of the company.

It's a wonderful system for those who can and do take advantage of it. The problem is that most of us aren't taught how to use this system on a consistent basis. In the next few pages I'll show you exactly how to harness this system and make it work in a way that helps you achieve your financial dreams, even if you're starting small.

First, let me say this: *Knowledge must come first, then results can follow.* The understanding of how money works is a definite prerequisite to realizing a significant level of financial success. A few of the concepts I'll be discussing may be new to you. Others may be familiar. What's certain is that reviewing them and internalizing them will be key to your increased success.

Even if you feel you have a handle on the topics I'm about to discuss, please study them with an open mind. You may get just one idea, but that idea could lead to enormous prosperity.

THE LAWS OF WEALTH

There's a fabulous book by George S. Clason that has really made a difference in my life. It's titled *The Richest Man in Babylon*, and I've read it dozens of times. If you haven't read this inspirational work on thrift and financial planning, I highly recommend it. If you have, you know how powerful it is. I found Clason's Five Laws of Gold to be especially useful, and I'd like to list them here for you now:

THE FIVE LAWS OF GOLD

1: Gold cometh gladly and in increasing quantity to any man who will put by not less than one-tenth of his earnings to create an estate for his future and that of his family.

2: Gold laboreth diligently and contentedly for the wise owner who finds for it profitable employment, multiplying even as the flocks of the field.

3: Gold clingeth to the protection of the cautious owner who invests it under the advice of men wise in its handling.

4: Gold slippeth away from the man who invests it in business or purposes with which he is not familiar or which are not approved by those skilled in its keep.

5: Gold flees the man who would force it to impossible earnings or who followeth the alluring advice of tricksters and schemers or who trusts it to his own inexperience and romantic desires in investment.

These laws are as true today as they were six thousand years ago in prosperous Babylon. If you read them carefully, you'll notice that only the first of the five laws pertains to saving and accumulating wealth through industry. The other four deal with proper and profitable management of wealth. It's not enough to accumulate massive sums of money. Money must be managed and put to positive use for the benefit of yourself as well as others.

Recall the biblical story of the three servants and the talents. The money was taken from the servant who had only one talent and given to the one who had ten. This tendency to "seek the best conditions for reproduction" is a universal law of money that applies to most other areas of nature as well. Everyone's heard, "It takes money to make money." I'm sure you'll agree there's a reason why. It may sometimes seem unfair, but money always goes to where it's treated best. This is particularly true in the world of investments. The markets are continually reacting to risk/reward trade-offs and seeking equilibrium.

The last three of Clason's Laws of Gold emphasize the importance of seeking guidance from those experienced in handling money. In other words, investing is a profession. If you aren't skilled in the financial markets and you have no intention of becoming an expert, hire someone capable of managing your nest egg properly. Most important, learn patience and let time work for you, not against you. Realize that time is your ally, and follow Wealth Ritual 4: **Employ your resources; money goes where it's treated best.**

The discussion that follows is intended to help you profitably manage your liquid investments—namely, stocks, bonds, and cash. (A liquid investment is one that can be converted immediately—or almost immediately—into available cash.) In general, your home or business would not be considered liquid because of the relatively lengthy time it takes to find a buyer.

Earlier we discussed saving a portion of your income for investments. That portion must be managed effectively and grown over time so that eventually it will provide for you and your needs *passively*, with earnings and dividends alone.

MARKET BASICS

STOCKS (OWNERSHIP)

I think it was Will Rogers who said, "Buy some good stock. Hold it until it goes up . . . and then sell it. If it doesn't go up, don't buy it!"

Ah, if only it were that easy.

When we discuss stocks, we're talking about ownership of an enterprise—equity in a corporation. A stock is nothing more than a certificate of ownership of shares in a company. Some companies are good investments, others are not so good. *Ultimately, the price your shares are worth is only what someone else will offer you for them.* Unfortunately, trying to predict how others will perceive a company's value can be tricky. There are many market factors that make buying individual stocks impractical for most individual investors. If you're investing for the long term, you can do well picking a few good companies and sticking with them. But if you're impatient, it's better to let a professional manage your equity investments.

Just how tricky the market is was brought home to me several years ago when I tried explaining the stock market to a class of third-graders. I was having a devil of a time until I hit upon something they could relate to. Realizing these little munchkins were well versed in sneaker brands, I began discussing some of the publicly traded athletic-shoe manufacturers: Nike (NKE), L.A. Gear (LA), and Reebok (RBK). I explained how good companies went up and bad companies went down and asked for a show of hands to select a winning stock.

Unanimously, the kids chose Nike. They explained to me that Michael Jordan was the greatest and that his endorsement of the shoes would send the common stock to stratospheric heights. Of course, I inwardly pooh-poohed this argument. I'd already bought and sold Nike about a year before for a near 50 percent profit and was too sophisticated to buy a stock that had already made that kind of move. I'd decided to wait for a pullback and buy the stock cheaper. At the time many of the analysts on the Street expected Nike's stock to mark time as L.A. Gear became the next big winner. Well, the end of the story is that L.A. Gear was disappointing, while Nike doubled in the next year and has continued to break new ground! I broke my own rule of not thinking long-term enough. I had tried to be smart and trade the stock. Consequently, I left a lot of money on the table. Those third-graders, though, would probably *still* own the stock. They weren't worried about being right all the time. They knew Nike was a good company, and that was that. They had faith in the system.

When investing in stocks, think long term and stick to your convictions. If you own a good company, stick with it until something changes. Selling a stock on the basis of price alone is a gamble. If the fundamentals of the company are sound, stay invested!

BONDS (LOANERSHIP)

A bond represents not ownership but rather an obligation (on the part of the borrower) to repay your invested amount at some predetermined point in the future. Think of a bond as you, the investor, loaning your money to a borrower. The borrower, or issuer, agrees to pay you a specified interest rate for the life of the bond and to repay your principal upon maturity. A bond represents "loanership." Consequently, bonds vary in quality, return, and duration, as well as risk.

Let me make a somewhat silly analogy: If you meet a total stranger on the street and he asks to borrow a $100 bill, would lending it be a safe bet? Probably not, but it depends on the time involved. If the stranger wants to borrow it for ten seconds so he can show his kid what Ben Franklin looks like, that may be a relatively safe bet. You might even consider loaning it to him if he promises to pay you 10 percent for the use of the money. If he wants to borrow it for thirty years, you might as well kiss it good-bye.

On the other hand, buying a U.S. government bond that matures in thirty years is probably a safe bet. I think the United States will be around to pay its debts in thirty years. Will the returns be the same in each of these scenarios? No way! Each situation has different risks associated with the promise to repay. The stranger may have to promise you 10 percent return for the use of your money for ten seconds. The U.S. government may promise you only a 6 percent annual return for use of your money for thirty years. All things being equal (including quality), the longer the maturity of the bond, the higher the return. However, it is still the free market (supply and demand) that ultimately determines the prices and rates of the bonds. Governments, municipalities, churches, schools, corporations, and— as I am currently discovering—even fraternities issue bonds to raise money to fund their operations.

MUTUAL FUNDS

For our purposes, a fund is a diversified collection of stocks or bonds that is professionally managed. If you join a mutual fund, *you* don't decide what stocks (or bonds) to buy or sell. A portfolio manager does that for you. The manager will take the money you deposit into the fund and manage it according to the fund's style and investment parameters. In return, you pay a small management fee for the professional advice and trading.

Most small investors participate in the market through mutual funds. They're convenient and relatively risk-free. You can diversify your investment among many different holdings without the time and expense of buying a few shares of many different companies. And best of all, diversification is the simplest way of reducing risk.

You are probably better off investing in mutual funds than trying to constantly trade your own portfolio—unless you crave the excitement of investing most of your nest egg in a few individual stocks and watching them go up and down. As we've discussed, I prefer to get my excitement in other ways than continually trading the market. Besides, if you can hire the best money managers on Wall Street, why waste your time? They'll beat the novice investor year in and year out.

In the last few pages of this section I'll introduce you to the best individual stock-picking method I know. It's conservative, virtually unknown, and has posted extraordinary returns. However, most individuals, and many professionals, don't have any type of investment opinion or methodology, and they make the mistake of selecting investments randomly or haphazardly. Even those who do their homework don't have a *consistent* qualitative method for choosing equities. This absence of a discipline is the number one reason investors fail to consistently make money in the market. The point is this: If you don't use my method or don't have one of your own, it's far better to piggyback a pro's strategy by using a mutual fund. Throughout this book I'll refer to mutual funds over and over again because they make the most sense for most people.

Stock and bond mutual funds vary in style, philosophy, risk, and return. The first variable that should be considered is risk. Are you comfortable with the style and types of issues that the fund will select? Would you feel better with blue-chip stocks, or can you be more aggressive? The table on page 139 discusses some of the most popular styles of mutual fund investing. In addition, I have included a fifteen-year track record (1975–1990) to illustrate how well each style of management would have performed. The performance numbers are based on the total ultimate value of $1 if invested in 1975 and held to

1990. The most risky styles are at the top, the most conservative near the bottom. The returns vary accordingly.

If you don't know which style suits you best, start out conservatively. It's better to err on the side of being too cautious than to lose sleep because the funds you chose are too volatile for your blood. Build your portfolio like you would a pyramid (we'll discussion the investment pyramid in more detail later). Make the base nice and sturdy with conservative investments, and take more and more risk with less and less money as you go up. Below is just one example of how to build a $100,000 portfolio:

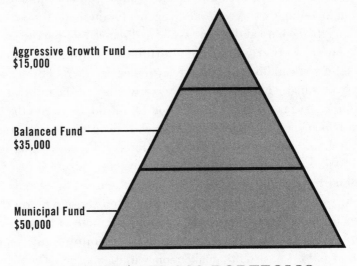

Aggressive Growth Fund — $15,000

Balanced Fund — $35,000

Municipal Fund — $50,000

SAMPLE $100,000 PORTFOLIO
OF MUTUAL FUNDS

Notice that my sample portfolio only has three funds in it. I see many people who have dozens of different funds for the sake of diversification. They forget that, by definition, a mutual fund *is* a diversified portfolio of securities. Having too many funds tends to create overdiversification. *If you diversify too much, your risk gets close to zero, but so does your return.* Three to five different mutual fund management styles or asset classes should give you a reasonably balanced portfolio. If you don't want to have more than one fund, you can find a "balanced" fund in which the manager divides your investment between several different asset classes. In today's world, the investor can hire

MUTUAL FUND STYLES OF INVESTING (1975–1990)

Style and Definition	Growth of $1 Invested at Year-End 1975
Small Stocks	
These are stocks in companies that are in the developing stages. They usually trade over-the-counter and may be thinly traded. These types of mutual funds seek long-term growth by investing in small companies that may have dynamic potential. These types of companies tend to be more volatile than larger and more seasoned companies.	$10.15
International	
Investments outside the U.S. are considered international investments. These can be in the bond market, the stock market, or both. In addition to the risks inherent in all securities, international funds are subject to the risks of currency exchange rate fluctuations.	$9.10
Aggressive Growth	
The investment objective of an aggressive-growth fund is capital appreciation. Some funds may use options or trade short-term in order to achieve higher returns.	$7.94
Growth and Income	
Growth funds invest in undervalued situations that have a solid record of paying dividends. Long-term capital gains are as important as dividend income.	$6.35
Balanced	
These portfolios have a mix of stocks, bonds, and cash. Their focus is on total return.	$5.81
Corporate Bonds	
The goal in a corporate-bond fund is to achieve a high level of income by investing in the debt of public corporations.	$4.01
Treasury Bills	
U.S. government bond funds seek safety and income.	$3.30
Municipal Bonds	
Municipal-bond portfolios seek tax-free income and safety by investing in high-quality state or local debt.	$2.40

SOURCE: Ibbottson Associates, per Shearson Lehman Brothers (paraphrased)

the best money managers available and access investment choices and conveniences that were once available only to the extremely wealthy. Use this to your advantage when building your portfolio.

THE DOW JONES INDUSTRIAL AVERAGE

The Dow is an average of thirty of the largest industrial stocks in the country. It's widely used as an indication of the market as a whole. Some question the validity of using the Dow as a representation of the market because it includes such a small number of securities. Others claim that the Standard & Poor's 500 (S&P 500) is a better indication of market direction because it profiles five hundred publicly traded companies. However, as we'll discuss later, *I believe that the Dow is the most important indice because it contains some of America's oldest publicly traded companies.* Most of them have been through every economic cycle the United States has known, including wars, recessions, and the Great Depression, while continuing to thrive and prosper. Consequently, all of the Dow components are considered "blue chips" because of their strength, stability, and staying power.

THE CASE FOR STOCKS

Everyone has a dream: a bigger home, a college education, secure retirement—maybe even a cattle ranch or a sports car. In pursuit of such goals, many investors have purchased common stocks and let public corporations work for *them.* You know I believe in owning part of your country's economic system, in taking risks and investing for your future by putting your money to work. You know how strongly I feel about making sure you use your economic power in a positive way to benefit others, create jobs, and help your nation prosper. All of these reasons are enough to invest in the great corporations of the world, but there's another reason to participate in the public financial markets: profit!

History has shown that the common stocks of public corporations have yielded higher returns than any other liquid asset class. The chart opposite represents the average annual returns of U.S. stocks, bonds, and cash for the last forty years.

40-YEAR AVERAGE ANNUAL TOTAL RETURN (1951–1990)

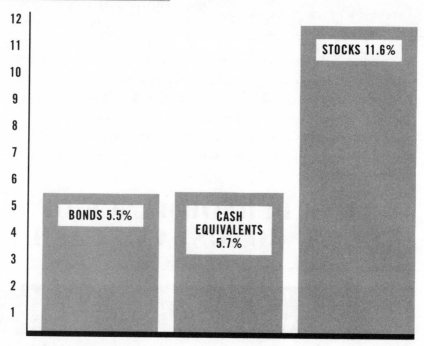

12	
11	STOCKS 11.6%
10	
9	
8	
7	
6	
5	
4	BONDS 5.5% CASH EQUIVALENTS 5.7%
3	
2	
1	

SOURCE: Merrill Lynch

As you can see, investing in stocks in the past has rewarded investors handsomely—almost double the return of bonds or cash equivalents. How important is a better return? Extremely! Based on this data, the table on page 142 shows the effects of habitually investing in either of these asset classes over the forty-year period.

The table on page 142 reveals that those who invested primarily in stocks over the past forty years obtained an investment result that dwarfs that of those who sunk their money into bonds or cash equivalents. The compounding effect is so dramatic that stock investors actually accumulated ten times the net worth of their bond-and-cash-investing counterparts. They obtained ten times the economic power, ten times the freedom, and probably a lot less financial strain simply because they chose to habitually trust the free enterprise system.

Is that type of reward worth the uncertainty of the equity markets? Most people would say yes. Especially when they consider that for the last twenty years inflation has averaged 6.3 percent (CPI according to Ibbotson and Associates). When inflation is factored out of bond and cash-equivalent investment results, there's very little left. Time and again, the lesson is demonstrated: Being too cautious in one's investment approach is the surest way to a zero return.

40 YEAR PERFORMANCE OF STOCKS, BONDS, AND CASH

AMOUNT INVESTED	Ending value after 40 years BONDS (5.5%)	Ending value after 40 years CASH (5.7%)	Ending value after 40 years STOCKS (11.6%)
$10,000 lump sum	$89,654	$97,240	$1,014,232
$100 a month	$84,263	$86,424	$1,038,502
$500 a month	$869,593	$918,321	$5,192,511
$1,000 a month	$1,739,186	$1,836,642	$10,385,021

Yet another graphic illustration of the wisdom of getting into the markets and staying there for the long term is provided in the following example. The University of Michigan conducted a study on the most recent five-year bull market—a period when stocks of U.S. corporations averaged a whopping 26.3 percent annual return to investors. The results are fascinating:

If you were out of the market for two months of the year, chances are your results were disappointing. Trying to predict the market—

when to invest and when to get out—proves almost impossible. The key to successful investing is having faith in the system, disregarding daily fluctuations, and dismissing fear and greed sensations that prompt emotional reactions. Also, as I've said: If you don't have the time and expertise to pick stocks like the pros, put your money into the hands of a professional mutual fund manager.

THE COST OF SHORT-TERM INVESTING
(UNIVERSITY OF MICHIGAN STUDY)

Bull Market of 1982–1987 (1,276 trading days)

Period of Investment	S&P 500 Annualized Return
Full 1,276 trading days	26.3%
Less the 10 biggest-gain days	18.3%
Less the 20 biggest-gain days	13.1%
Less the 30 biggest-gain days	8.5%
Less the 40 biggest-gain days	4.3%

THE ULTIMATE WEALTH-BUILDING TOOL: DOLLAR COST AVERAGING

The biggest fear people have in investing in the market is that they'll buy at the wrong time. Nothing is more discouraging than buying a stock, bond, or mutual fund just before the market gods decide it's time for a pullback. You make your investment on Friday, and by Tuesday the price has headed south for the winter. Even a tiny price drop can dampen your spirits—after all, you've given up a lot to make that investment. Maybe you put off an important purchase; minimally, you've denied yourself a certain degree of devil-may-care spending. If only the market gods would tell you the exact day the stock (market, fund, etc.) would go up, you'd put your money to work just in time. But there's no such thing as just-in-time investing. Markets do fluctuate, and the only device I've seen that comes close to eliminating price-fluctuation risk (and is practical for individual investors) is an investment discipline called **dollar cost averaging.**

With dollar cost averaging you eliminate market timing risks by investing a fixed amount of money at regular intervals. For example, instead of investing $15,000 today and hoping you bought low, you can invest, say, $3,000 every month for the next five months. You can invest weekly, monthly, quarterly, or yearly. Any interval will work as long as it's consistent. This strategy works well if you're starting small—with, say, $100 to $300 a month—since you can invest a little bit as you get paid.

Dollar cost averaging is designed to let you profit in up, down, sideways, and volatile markets. It works because you're always buying some shares in down markets at the cheaper price. In most cases, you'll need a full market cycle (about five years) to get the full benefit of this strategy. Carefully examine the following hypothetical scenarios. They're based on a $300-a-month investment for five months in different market environments.

From the table opposite you can see that in virtually every type of market, dollar cost averaging is better than investing your money all at once. So if you think you're at a disadvantage because you don't have a huge amount to invest, you're not. *Over time, dollar cost averaging is probably the most powerful investing tool you can have at your disposal.* In all cases, your average cost per share is less than the last (end) price in the market. In the up-market scenario, you would have paid more than if you'd invested the entire $1,500 at the beginning price. However, you'd still wind up with a $14.05-per-share profit and would have reduced your risk had the shares not gone up. You also would have achieved a cost basis $4.05 below the average market price. It may seem smarter, in hindsight, to have invested all at once in the up market, however I don't know anyone who can predict such markets accurately. *The idea is not to try to predict and gamble on the market direction but to win in any market environment.* In the down-market scenario you're under water but at an average cost of $15 as opposed to $25 had you invested all $1,500 at once. The last price of $5 is unfortunate, but you've cut an 80 per-

THE EFFECTS OF MARKET ENVIRONMENTS USING DOLLAR COST AVERAGING

U p Market

REGULAR INVESTMENT	SHARE PRICE	SHARES ACQUIRED
$300	$5.00	60
$300	10.00	30
$300	15.00	20
$300	20.00	15
$300	25.00	12
$1,500	TOTALS	137
Average share price (75/5)	$15.00	
Average purchase price using dollar cost averaging ($1,500/137)	$10.95	

D own Market

REGULAR INVESTMENT	SHARE PRICE	SHARES ACQUIRED
$300	$25.00	12
$300	20.00	15
$300	15.00	20
$300	10.00	30
$300	5.00	60
$1,500	TOTALS	137
Average share price (75/5)	$15.00	
Average purchase price using dollar cost averaging ($1,500/137)	$10.95	

(continued)

Sideways Market

REGULAR INVESTMENT	SHARE PRICE	SHARES ACQUIRED
$300	$12.00	25
$300	10.00	30
$300	12.00	25
$300	10.00	30
$300	12.00	25
$1,500	TOTALS	135
Average share price (56/5)	$11.20	
Average purchase price using dollar cost averaging ($1,500/135)	$11.11	

Volatile Market

REGULAR INVESTMENT	SHARE PRICE	SHARES ACQUIRED
$300	$10.00	30
$300	5.00	60
$300	10.00	30
$300	25.00	12
$300	15.00	20
$1,500	TOTALS	152
Average share price (65/5)	$13	
Average purchase price using dollar cost averaging ($1,500/152) ($1,500/137)	$9.86	

Summary of Results
Dollar Cost Averaging Strategy

Total investment: $1,500 ($300/month for 5 months)

MARKET TYPE	BEG. PRICE	END PRICE	AVG. PRICE	AVG. COST	SHARES ACQUIRED
Up	$5.00	$25.00	$15.00	$10.95	137
Down	25.00	5.00	15.00	10.95	137
Sideways	12.00	12.00	11.20	11.11	135
Volatile	10.00	15.00	13.00	9.86	152

cent loss in half! The worst possible case is that you average down to zero, but at least you've played defense to some extent.

Dollar cost averaging will soften the blow a bit if your investment goes down, but if you do see a trend in which you're steadily losing ground, there's probably a reason why and that investment should be reviewed. Long-term investing and dollar cost averaging don't entirely eliminate the need to consistently monitor your investment portfolio. They're tools, after all—not magic wands. In most cases, just practicing a discipline, any discipline, can help you avoid making emotionally charged and costly mistakes.

HOW IMPORTANT IS DEFENSE?

One of the most important rules of investing is that capital preservation should always exceed capital appreciation. In other words, the most important consideration is how much risk you're taking with your principal. You must invest with the idea of potential return in mind; however, you should be conservative enough to keep your principal as safe as possible. To illustrate the importance of playing defense, see the example on page 148.

As you can see, one bad year can reduce your performance substantially. In the example, your investment performance for the first three years was good—15 percent. The problem came in the fourth year, when you lost 15 percent of your portfolio value. By itself that

HOW IMPORTANT
IS DEFENSE?

YEAR 1	YEAR 2	YEAR 3	YEAR 4	Average Annual Compound Return
+15%	+15%	+15%		+15%
+15%	+15%	+15%	-15%	6.6%

doesn't seem bad, since you had three good years. However, that one off year causes your average annual return for the four-year period to drop to 6.6 percent, effectively negating the previous three years' hard work.

Consistency in returns is most important. What's shocking is that, were your goal to get your returns back up to the previous 15 percent average (for the five-year period), you'd have to find some way to get a stellar performance out of year five. In fact, you'd have to earn over 55 percent that year to achieve a five-year average of 15 percent. If you hadn't had the down year, you would have needed only 15 percent to keep the same average.

So it's important to keep your guard up every single year. I have people calling me all the time wanting to gamble on rumors and penny stocks. Their justification is that they'll "play" with just the little bit they can afford to lose. After all, they can only lose what they've invested. I think this approach is ridiculous! If you have to gamble, go to Vegas and leave serious investment professionals alone. As a broker, I find nothing more insulting than a client's placing a small order for a long shot. Usually it's a stock no one has ever heard of and no one ever will.

I almost never take orders for stocks I don't recommend. Recently, I've noticed that the gamblers have developed a special affection for what I call "petri-dish stocks." Stay away from these types of speculative issues. They're usually generated by companies that have one revolutionary product or drug that will save the world if it works. They're betting their livelihood on this one product, and if they succeed, the investor will have a home run. However, if someone in a lab somewhere drops the petri dish, the stock's price disappears into the abyss.

Believe me, if the revolutionary products these companies boast about were sure things, they'd have no trouble finding private investors, instead of using the public market. Maintaining your wealth is of utmost importance. Don't be afraid to make a well-thought-out investment—just don't get careless and forget to play defense.

THE INVESTMENT PYRAMID

With good reason, many finance experts liken building a portfolio of investments to building a pyramid. The base should be large and sturdy, consisting of safe, secure investments. As you near the top of the pyramid, you should take more and more risk with smaller and smaller amounts of money. The following illustration gives you a clear picture of what I'm talking about. Most people should avoid putting money in the tip-top, speculative section of the pyramid. Speculative investing tends to consume a lot of time because it requires frequent, by-the-seat-of-the-pants decisions. Also, except for a few brilliant investors, most people who dabble in this area don't extract much in the way of returns. To be sure, many are cavalier about it. They liken speculative investing to gambling and *expect* to lose money—it's their Las Vegas or the lottery. If they win, they can win big. But usually they're just throwing their money away. As I've said, I prefer to entertain myself in other ways than losing money. I hope you'll choose to do the same.

The investment pyramid should give you a good idea of how to build your portfolio. If you're just starting out, stay relatively conservative. Once your nest egg begins to grow and you gain more investment experience, you can "edge" up the pyramid in search of higher returns, incurring a higher degree of risk. The most important thing is to develop a mix that makes you feel comfortable; after all, it's *your* money.

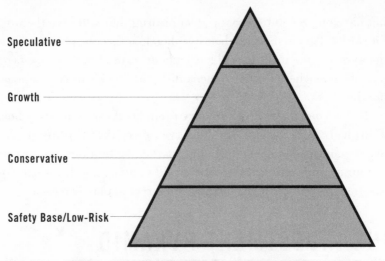

Speculative

Growth

Conservative

Safety Base/Low-Risk

THE INVESTMENT PYRAMID

SPECULATIVE: Commodities, options and futures, speculative common stocks, junk bonds.

GROWTH: Growth common stocks, growth mutual funds, some corporate and municipal bonds.

CONSERVATIVE: High-quality common stocks, preferred stocks, utility stocks, conservative mutual funds, investment-grade corporate and municipal bonds, long-term U.S. Treasury bonds.

SAFETY BASE/LOW-RISK: Money market funds, certificates of deposit (CDs), short- and moderate-term U.S. Treasury securities.

THE RULE OF 72

The Rule of 72 is an approximation of how long it will take to double your money at various rates of return, and it can be extremely useful in planning your financial future. Actually seeing the differences that a higher rate of return can make is staggering. To answer the question "How long will it take my money to double at this rate of return?" just divide 72 by the rate of return you anticipate receiving. For example, at 10 percent your money will double in 7.2 years. The chart on the facing page should give you an idea of how powerful this tool can be.

I use the Rule of 72 to make ballpark estimates of what the compounding effect on my money will be. For example, if I have $10,000

THE RULE OF 72

RETURN	YEARS TO DOUBLE
1%	72
2%	36
4%	18
6%	12
8%	9
10%	7.2
12%	6
15%	4.8
18%	4
24%	3

(72 / 10 = 7.2 years)

and expect to get a 10 percent return, I can predict that in 7.2 years my money will have doubled to $20,000. At that same rate after 14.4 years my money will have doubled again to $40,000.

If you're not satisfied with general estimates but want exact figures, there is a compound-interest table in the back of this book (Exhibit 4) based on the future value of $1. If you're investing $5,000, just multiply the future value of $1 by 5,000.

THE COMMON MISTAKE

Let's take up again the subject of risk. Most people I talk to suffer from riskaphobia. Nothing scares them more than risking their hard-earned savings. They'd rather have a root canal every day than risk losing one cent of their principal. This is usually the result of a grave misunderstanding of risk. The fact is, we've been taught to fear it. What we haven't been taught is the definition of what is risky. The truth is that life is a risk. And, as I've said before, doing nothing is a risk—perhaps the greatest risk of all. John F. Kennedy said it best: "There are risks and costs associated with a program of action. But they are less than the long-range risks and costs of comfortable inaction."

The point is, *those investors who don't want to take even a small risk will find that it's only a matter of time before they're put into a corner and forced to make a decision they'd rather not make and take chances they'd normally not have to take.* Eventually, inflation and taxes will erode their savings away. Unless they die first, they'll have to decide either to lower their standard of living or take great risks to preserve it. Usually by this point the risk is too great and their dreams are shattered as well as their dignity.

If this sounds melodramatic, recall the fact that at age sixty-five or older only 2 percent of the U.S. population is self-sustaining. Since the employment rate in America is over 95 percent, one can only conclude that most of these people worked hard and led fully productive lives, only to have their dreams evaporate simply because they failed to act.

Typically, what investors loathe most is volatility, and what they love more than anything is safety. The fact is, volatility is their best friend, and safety is their enemy.

Certificates of deposit (CDs), for example, have long been thought to be the U.S. investor's best friend. They pay a market rate of interest, and they're 100 percent insured (up to $100,000 each) by the F.D.I.C. Most people love investing in CDs because they're safe. Well, I'm here to say that there's nothing absolutely safe in this whole world, and you get exactly what you pay for. If you take no risk, you get no return—that's the way life works. Besides, as we've already discussed, after you factor out taxes and inflation from your return, you probably end up in the hole. And here's the worst part: Even though CDs carry a guaranteed fixed rate of interest, the rate changes daily. As an investor, you've got to try and catch the highest rate and lock up your money for a long time. You also may incur a penalty for early withdrawal. Because of this guessing game, most CD investors deposit their money for a six-month or one-year period and roll it over when it matures. In other words, they don't know what rate they'll get in a year when their investment comes due. They justify this by knowing that if they need their money, they can have it when the CD matures. They're "liquid," all right.

Let me show you the price they pay, in terms of risk, for this so-called liquidity.

The historical graph below represents the average six-month CD rates since 1969. Please answer this question: Does this represent a secure, stable investment or a volatile (risky) investment?

AVERAGE RATES ON A 6-MONTH CD 1969–1993

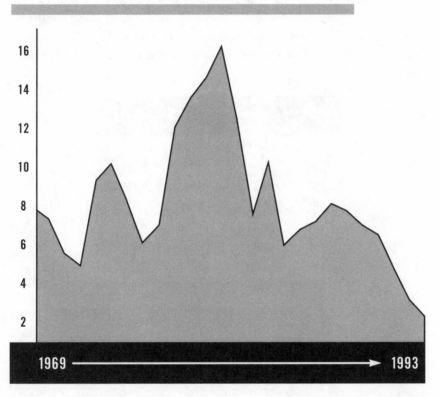

If you'd invested in a six-month CD in 1969 and renewed it every six months, your returns would have varied this widely. That's volatility! Imagine if you were retired and living off the income interest from a CD. Your monthly income would go up and down like a yo-yo! If you'd invested $100,000 and rates were 9 percent, you'd get about $750 a month in income for that six-month period. However, if rates dropped to 5 percent, your income would decline to about $416 a month. I don't know anyone who'd be happy to take a 45 percent cut in salary, yet that's exactly what millions of people do when they put their faith in CD rates.

I've said it before in this book, but I'll say it again: If you do nothing, you'll receive nothing. When someone offers you an investment with absolute safety, a good return, no thought or effort on your part, and no charges, you'd better take a look from a different angle. I don't think that's being negative, that's being realistic. I've heard it said that by investing for income in CDs you are, in effect, betting your standard of living on the whims of inflation. I couldn't agree more. The data below was used to create the six-month CD graph you just saw:

6-MONTH CD RATES			
1969	7.91%	1982	12.57%
1970	7.65	1983	9.27
1971	5.21	1984	10.68
1972	5.02	1985	8.25
1973	8.31	1986	6.50
1974	9.98	1987	7.01
1975	6.89	1988	7.85
1976	5.62	1989	9.08
1977	5.92	1990	9
1978	8.61	1991	7
1979	11.44	1992	5
1980	12.99	1993	3
1981	15.77		

Annualized average monthly rates.
SOURCE: 1969–1989 Federal Reserve Board; 1990–1993 author's experience

At the risk of beating a dead horse, let me illustrate this point about the unworthiness of CDs as a long-term investment in a slightly different way. If you were retired and relying on income from a $100,000 CD for the past twenty-four years, here's how your income (based on the same data) would have bounced around:

THE CD SALARY-REDUCTION PLAN

YEAR	MONTHLY INCOME
1969	$659
1971	$434
1973	$693
1975	$574
1977	$493
1980	$1,083
1984	$890
1989	$757
1993	$250 (estimated)

Keep in mind that this table doesn't consider inflation and loss of purchasing power. For example: $659 a month in 1969 was a pretty good income—the equivalent of about $2,125 a month today, assuming 5 percent inflation. In other words, if you retired in 1969 with a $100,000 CD and you've lived off the interest income for the past twenty-four years, by the time you get to 1993 your income, in purchasing power, is roughly 12 percent of what it was in 1969. No wonder we see so many older people going back to work!

1978: IT WAS A VERY GOOD YEAR

To make a point in my seminars about there never being a "perfect" time to invest, I often take the attendees back a couple of decades to the year 1978. Some of the major American newspaper headlines of the year were:

37 ISRAELIS SLAIN IN PLO RAID ON HAIFA BUS

CARTER DEFERS NEUTRON BOMB

SOUTH KOREAN AIRLINER IS FORCED DOWN IN RUSSIA

"BUGS" ARE DISCOVERED IN U.S. EMBASSY IN MOSCOW

POPE PAUL VI DIES, JOHN PAUL I IS ELECTED

JOHN PAUL I DIES, POLISH CARDINAL IS NAMED SUCCESSOR

900 AMERICAN CULT MEMBERS COMMIT SUICIDE IN GUYANA

OPEC RAISES PRICES 14%

CITY OF CLEVELAND DEFAULTS

U.S. INFLATION RATE: 12.4%; PRIME RATE 12%

With all of the turbulent events taking place in 1978, it was very hard to be positive about America's economic future. To invest one's hard-earned money in the stock market seemed almost ludicrous. Throw in my tragic fifth-grade loss of the city spelling bee on the word *echoes* (not to mention my hopes for a motorbike as a reward for winning the contest), and you've described an agonizing year. If Americans ever had a time to get down on the American Dream, it was 1978. However, we lived through it. In fact, the United States actually grew and prospered.

The truth is, there'll always be some reason to fear the market: war, inflation, world unrest, a new president—the list goes on. There are very few, if any, times when all lights are green. Given that, it makes sense to plunge in as soon as you can.

To underscore the point, let's say that in 1978 you were particularly brave and faithful and decided to invest $10,000 in the Dow Jones industrials. Today that $10,000 would be worth over $44,000! That's over four times your original investment—enough to overcome inflation and have some healthy growth as well. In terms of investing in the market, 1978 actually turned out to be a very good year!

In 1978 the Dow Jones Industrial Average had a low of 807 points and a high of 893. *As of 1995 the Dow Jones has recently bumped the*

4,000 mark for the first time in history!

Conclusion: You need to get over the fear of current events and look at the bigger picture. Don't let the daily negative news stories scare you into indecision. Being immobilized will hurt you in the long run. As I've said repeatedly in this book, the one thing that's always worked to the advantage of the investor is time combined with compound interest. You must think and invest for the long term.

> **Take calculated risks. That is quite different from being rash.**
> —GENERAL GEORGE S. PATTON

WHY NOT?

As you know by now, I believe that successful investing depends on a long-term strategy that includes stock investments, not timing the peaks and valleys of the market. I hope you find many reasons to invest now, but if you're still thinking of reasons *not* to invest, consider the reasons that have kept others out of the market in the past. I'm sure there are some similarities to today's excuses. The illustration on page 158 shows what $10,000 invested in the U.S. market each year, without adjusting for inflation, would be worth today.

Since we can't see the future, we must use the past as our guide. Historically, the stock market has always gone up. Even after the Great Depression and two world wars, it continues to reach new highs. What more do you need? Make a resolution today to set aside your fears and concerns and have faith in a proven system.

TO TRADE OR NOT TO TRADE?

Let me begin this discussion with a question: *Have you ever heard of anyone or do you know anyone who's amassed a fortune trading stocks?* In my career I've had the opportunity to meet many members of the financial elite, and I have never known a soul to make a fortune by trading alone. I'm reminded of a line once uttered by William Travers, an American attorney who often exaggerated his stutter to

Year	Why *Not* to Invest	Value Today of $10,000 Invested Then
1972	When the market drops 29 points in one day, I stay away!	$99,641
1973	DOW reaches 1,000 for the first time—a crash is due.	$83,759
1974	OPEC is in control—Nixon isn't.	$98,159
1975	The ugliest market in 40 years!	$133,400
1976	New York City nears bankruptcy.	$97,125
1977	Inflation is 12 percent, coffee is $5 a pound.	$78,450
1978	The market has been flat for two years.	$84,523
1979	Interest rates are way too high—the economy can't take it.	$79,346
1980	Iran holds hostages; hold your cash!	$66,990
1981	Chrysler needs $400 million; look out, market!	$50,578
1982	The recession has started—maybe depression.	$53,175
1983	Ten percent unemployment and bank failures.	$43,763
1984	Dow at 1,250, new high; I'll wait for a pullback.	$35,740
1985	More bank failures than the thirties.	$33,645
1986	Federal deficit is over $200 billion.	$25,558
1987	Black Monday strikes!	$21,546
1988	Chilling effect continues. Stay out of stocks!	$20,479
1989	S&L's need bailing out.	$17,579
1990	New decade, old junk-bond problems.	$13,359
1991	War with Iraq. Things couldn't be worse.	$13,789
1992	Recession lingers, new president elected.	$10,580

SOURCE: Edward D. Jones & Co., as seen in *The Wall Street Journal* (paraphrased)

beef up his witty comments. Travers was in a group of people watching the end of a yacht race at Newport in the mid-1800s. As boat after boat glided across the finish line, each owner's name was announced. Upon learning that every single yacht belonged to a wealthy stockbroker, Travis exclaimed, "And w-w-where are the c-c-customers' yachts?"

There's a big difference between trading and investing. In this book I've emphasized the benefits of long-term *investing*. *Trading* implies short-term, risky decision making where the investor switches investments almost as often as he changes his clothes, or more. I've studied trading methodology for years; I'm familiar with most of the current "hot" philosophies, and some of them do work—for a time. However, there is only one thing that has always worked: investing for the long term.

Jesse Lauriston Livermore, a stock market speculator who lived and traded early in the century, is remembered as one of the greatest traders who ever lived. He was so well respected that just the hint of Jesse Livermore favoring a particular security sent ripples through the market. It's widely believed that he authored the legendary book *Reminiscences of a Stock Operator*, first published in 1923, using the pen name Edwin Lefevre. Supposedly he used a pen name to avoid "shocking" the markets with his trading secrets.

In his book, a bible among Wall Street traders, Jesse reveals his intimate thoughts and trading strategies. As he grows more and more experienced, his skill increases as does the size of his "investments." He tells of fabulous cruises and a fast-lane lifestyle, but always the market interrupts his vacations. He is drawn to it, addicted to the numbers. He doesn't see the numbers as the share prices of publicly traded America; he only sees that the numbers move, and with that movement is a chance for profit.

Because he was in essence a gambler, Jesse Livermore was wealthy and impoverished many times in his life. Ironically—or perhaps, predictably—he died broke.

In talking with others about *Reminiscences of a Stock Operator*, I've realized that I'm one of the few who doesn't see the wisdom in Jesse's trading approach. It seems foolish to spend so much time trying to predict the future—plotting which numbers will advance and which will decline. Yet nearly every broker I talk to seems in awe of

Livermore's trading prowess. My typical comeback is: "Yeah, but he died broke."

Typically, Jesse lost everything he had when the market turned against him, but being a lifelong student of the market, he responded by mentally logging the experience in order to learn from it. Thereupon, he would execute his "new" trading methodology to the letter, but ultimately he would lose his money because of some unforeseen variable.

Clearly, Jesse Livermore's great mistake was in believing that the market is, in the short term, a predictable machine.

There are many market-timing services and trading methodologies one can follow. As I've said, some of them do work at times. But what of it? As the saying goes, even a broken clock is right twice a day. The problem is that even if a given methodology does work, you've got to be right twice—consecutively. First, your timing has to be perfect when you buy. Second, you've got to know precisely when to sell. Believe me, that's tough!

Also, once a certain methodology becomes accepted and everyone uses the same discipline, there's no volatility because everyone is buying and selling according to the same parameters. It takes differences of opinions to make markets. If you think you should sell a stock, there has to be someone else who's equally convinced it should be bought.

Think about it: If a trading methodology worked every time, it would never be packaged and sold—it would be far too valuable to be spread around. Ultimately, the only person who usually makes money trading is the broker, who gets a commission for every buy and sell. As a serious investor, not a gambler, forget the esoteric forms of market wizardry and invest for the long term—you'll be better off.

Besides, if you can get double-digit returns in a mutual fund, without smoke and mirrors, do it and go fishing. It's more fun.

THINKING LONG TERM

In my experience on Wall Street I have been exposed to many different investment strategies, vehicles, and packaged securities. All of these creations are designed to meet investors' specific needs. Some do and some don't. Some have track records, some are experimental, and some are lousy but sellable. Almost everyone in this business has an opinion on the market and an investment philosophy. Some of these opinions are very good and come from educated, well-respected people. Others are dismissable.

Recently I perused an investment best-seller, which explained, in detail, one broker's formula for success. It revealed his personal trading secrets and probably sold a million copies and earned its author many new clients. However, in the book the broker actually apologizes to his clients for his past performance, because their losses were substantial. Further, he concedes that he never does business with anyone he knows socially for fear of jeopardizing the relationship.

In my opinion, there's something wrong with a strategy that a broker feels comfortable hawking in a book but uncomfortable sharing with the people he cares about most. I'm sure this broker means well. But apparently the only way to get famous anymore is to build a fancier mousetrap and sell it, even if it doesn't work.

About a year ago an associate and I called a broker in New York and asked him for his stock recommendations. He gave us about a dozen stock picks, based on his methodology. To date the portfolio is in a loss position, while the averages are making new highs. While it's not entirely fair to judge someone's performance on the basis of a one-year yardstick, a more reliable indicator, such as five or ten years, becomes irrelevant in rendering a verdict on a given stock guru's strategy. By the time the numbers confirm the guru's all wet, he's collected a million dollars in book royalties and another guru has risen to the fore.

The fact is, most "hot investment strategies" are fads, gimmicks. People want something new and exciting. Old seems boring, even if it works. Long-term investing isn't state-of-the-art. But—listen up, folks—*the only strategy that has always worked is investing for the long term.*

I suggest that you faithfully stick to the fundamentals. If you choose a good stock mutual fund that invests for the long term and leave it alone, you'll be far better off than if you jump from idea to idea. Alternatively, you can invest in a Dow or S&P 500 index fund (which offers wide diversity by purchasing shares in each of the companies listed in the index). Most brokerage firms offer index funds these days, and if you aren't good at making decisions, buying the index look-alike will probably get you to where you want to go. Experts estimate that 75 percent of the professional money managers on Wall Street fail to outperform the S&P 500 on a consistent basis. If you own a portfolio that mirrors the index, you've beaten most of the professionals, without one minute's research on your part.

I'm not suggesting that you can't beat the index, or that you can't find a mutual fund that will give you superior performance. I know many ways to get excellent performance, and I try to show my clients the best returns available. Every year new hot-shot money managers enter the scene, and some of them are truly very good. But I've found that most small investors don't aspire to be earnings superstars—they just want a reasonable return so they can pursue other interests. If that's your outlook, don't sweat it. Stick to a consistent, long-term approach, and you'll reach your dreams. And if you don't have an approach yet, I'll share with you shortly my personal method for long-term investing that has worked better than the indices and most of the professionals.

Roger Ibbotson, of Ibbotson and Associates, is considered the foremost expert in the area of statistical securities research. In affiliation with the University of Chicago's Graduate School of Securities Research, he released a study that I think is quite remarkable. The analysts went back to 1925 and put aside $1 in four different places: Inflation (CPI), thirty-year U.S. Treasury bonds, index of corporate bonds, and the S&P 500. In 1992 they theoretically opened the box to see the effects of time on each of these indices.

As you can see, the dollar invested in the S&P 500 is almost twenty times more valuable than the corporate bonds and over seventy times more valuable than the inflation-adjusted dollar. Significantly, the dollar set aside in the S&P 500 actually only grew to $25.89; the remainder of the asset growth can be attributed to the effect of compounding. Over two-thirds of the return is attributed to dividend accumulation, reinvestment, and compounding over time! So successful investing is not a matter of which new theory is hot lately, or when to buy low and when to sell high. It's a matter of

EFFECTS OF TIME ON $1

University of Chicago Graduate School of Research

	1925	1992
Inflation (CPI)	$1	$7.46
30-year Treasury	$1	$17.99
Corporate bonds	$1	$27.18
S&P 500	$1	$517.50

SOURCE: Ibbotson and Associates, per Putnam Funds Group

getting invested, staying invested, and reinvesting the dividends over time. The accumulation of wealth is virtually that simple if you side with time.

The difficult part is being patient and not letting emotion get in the way. I've found a questionnaire that seems to help my clients avoid making emotionally charged decisions. Before you make any type of investment, I encourage you to ask yourself these questions and share your answers with your financial advisor.

SMART QUESTIONS TO ASK YOURSELF BEFORE MAKING ANY INVESTMENT

- What is my time horizon?
- What is my target return on this investment?
- Do I want to buy low and sell high, or buy high and sell low?
- What are my priorities, by rank?
  _____Performance
  _____Service
  _____To feel good, smart, or savvy
- How many months of negative return am I willing to withstand in order to achieve my goal?

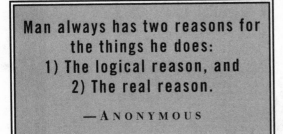

I think it's important to get clear on your objectives before making any investment. After you have completed this questionnaire, keep it with your other financial documents. Whenever you start to decide to sell or make any changes to this investment, review your questionnaire and ask yourself: *Am I making this decision based on my objectives, or is it based on my emotions of fear and greed?* Have I achieved my objectives? Am I acting in accordance with my priorities?

If your first priority is to feel smart or savvy—in particular, to feel like a market player—then you may have the need to call your broker every day and talk about the market. If you need to feel decisive, you may want to trade every day. Understand that this is probably not the best way to achieve optimum performance, but if you choose to feel good in that way, return is not your priority. If your priority is performance, you'll want to think long term and disregard daily fluctuations. If your priority is service, then you want someone to be there to hold your hand when things are tough. You want someone to return your calls immediately and help you understand your monthly statement. If you care this much about service, performance is secondary. Any priority is okay; just understand what it is you expect from your investments and your financial advisor.

If you truly desire performance, then you'll need to have a longer time horizon. You may go months without looking at the daily quotes. That's fine—you're not interested in quick fixes. *If you start to feel the urge to make some changes and you don't know why, go back to your questionnaire.* If you want to sell your investment because it's down a few points, go back to the question of whether or not you wish to buy low, sell high or buy high, sell low. You may laugh because this is such a silly question. No one wants to buy high and sell low, but that's exactly what you're about to do because you're emotionally disgusted with the stock. Believe me, I've made this mistake often enough to be considered an expert. Don't get caught up in the emotion. Fall back on your original objectives, and you are sure to do the right thing.

THE BEST-KEPT SECRET ON WALL STREET: THE TOP 10 INVESTMENT STRATEGY

In the next few pages I'd like to share with you a summary of *the single best stock market investment methodology I've ever seen*—and I've done my homework over the years. I know you'll benefit tremendously, as I have, from this high-quality, high-return, low-risk investment strategy. Lest you accuse me of being one of those here-today-gone-tomorrow gurus I mentioned before, complete with his own surefire plan for making a short-term killing in the market, let me tell you that I didn't invent this strategy, nor is it short-term.

Even so, I know a good thing when I see it. Many professionals have practiced this method for years with incredible success. As far as I can tell, this simple, disciplined, and effective philosophy for investing in common stocks has been around for years but has remained undiscovered by individual investors. It has been highlighted in financial publications such as *Fortune, Money, The New York Times, Barron's, Kiplinger's Personal Finance Magazine*, and the *Financial Times*, to name a few, and it has performed excellently. The best part is that you can achieve the same results as the pros with only one minute's research and homework per year! It's that good.

This method is profound in its simplicity, yet it works remarkably well. Michael O'Higgins, author of *Beating the Dow*, says: "People tend to complicate something in direct proportion to its importance." I agree totally. Since money is an important subject for most people, Wall Street has bombarded the investing public with sophisticated computer-trading models and impressive market technobabble. Consequently, people have a hard time believing that simple is what works.

The only difficult parts of this method are convincing yourself not to meddle with the proven strategy and coping with the boredom of it.

If you're willing to forgo exciting cocktail-party bragging about your stock market maneuver of the day in favor of real, consistent asset growth, then read on. My idea of fun is beating the pros at their own game, even if it is common sense!

THE PHILOSOPHY

As the most popular market index, The Dow Jones Industrial Average (DJIA)* is a weighted average of thirty of some of the most widely held, widely analyzed, and widely followed public companies in the world. In a sense, the Dow *is* the market. The Top 10 approach focuses solely on these thirty stocks. They become our universe, from which all of our stocks will be selected. Why?

To answer that question, let me ask another question: Why search the four corners of the earth for performance when the best-quality issues, the ones that consistently outperform most of the pros, are right here under our nose—in the Dow 30? Look at this list of the steady companies that make up the Dow. You'll probably recognize most of them.

THE BLUE-CHIP 30 DOW INDUSTRIALS

AlliedSignal	Goodyear
ALCOA	IBM
American Express	International Paper
AT&T	McDonald's
Bethlehem Steel	Merck
Boeing	J. P. Morgan
Caterpillar	Philip Morris
Chevron	Procter & Gamble
Coca-Cola	Sears
Disney	Texaco
DuPont	3M
Eastman Kodak	Union Carbide
Exxon	United Technologies
General Electric	Westinghouse
General Motors	Woolworth

As you can see, most of these companies are household names. They're the biggest and best that America, and maybe the world, has to offer. Together, these thirty companies employ nearly five million people and have assets of over a trillion dollars. Their combined sales exceed the gross national product (GNP) of every country in the

*Dow Jones Industrial Average is the property of Dow Jones & Company, Inc., which is unaffiliated with and has not participated in any way in the creation of this strategy, a portfolio, or the selection of its stocks.

world except the United States, the Soviet Union, Japan, and maybe China. These issues are considered blue chips because of their size and longevity. With companies of this stature, there appears to be long-term opportunity with very little risk. To me it makes sense to select a portfolio from these quality issues.

THE STRATEGY: KEEPING IT SIMPLE

This strategy is based on the following premises:

1. Common stocks are the smartest long-term-growth investment alternative.
2. The Dow stocks are solid blue-chip companies of enormous economic importance, and *all* tend to make good long-term investments.
3. A portfolio of out-of-favor Dow stocks has outperformed the Dow Jones Industrial Average consistently on an annual basis—an achievement that has eluded the majority of professional money managers.

The Top 10 strategy simply uses one indicator of value: yield. How does this work?

First, let me explain the concept of *dividend yield*, or "yield" as we'll refer to it. Most companies in the Dow average (twenty-nine out of thirty at this time) pay a return to their shareholders in the form of a *dividend*. Usually this dividend comes from the company's earnings, and it's a way of paying the shareholders for the use of their money. It can be $1, $2, or $5 per share, or more, or less. But the dollar value doesn't matter that much. What's important is the dollar value of the dividend paid to the shareholder with respect to the share price of the company's common stock. This relationship gives us the dividend yield.

Let me give you an example: Let's say that XYZ Company is trading for $20 per share, and the dividend it pays you, the shareholder, is $1 per share. Regardless of how many shares you own or how much money you've invested, your percentage return, on dividends alone, would be 5 percent. (1/20 = .05) That's clear enough, right?

On the other hand, let's say that XYZ Company has dropped to $5 per share, and the dividend it pays the shareholder is still $1 per share. Now your percentage return, on dividends alone, would be 20 percent (1/5 = .20). Clear again?

So, as the price moves up and down, the yield fluctuates equally in the opposing direction, like the two ends of a seesaw. And when the yield is high, the stock is low. We use this mathematical relationship to our advantage and *buy only those companies with high yields and, consequently, relatively low prices.* It's discount shopping!

I realize that's *not* the way most people are used to measuring return on stocks. Typically, they calculate return on the basis of how much a company's shares appreciate. For example, you buy one share of XYZ for $20, and over the course of, say, a year it appreciates to $25. You now have a $5, or 25 percent, profit in terms of *price appreciation.*

But a distinction needs to be made. There are two parts to the return an investor realizes when investing in dividend-paying stocks: dividend yield and price appreciation. Both are important. Together they form a measure of performance called *total return.* That's what we're after, and this Top 10 strategy considers both. Most people focus all their attention on whether their share price is going up. That's a big mistake! If you recall one of our earlier examples, you'll remember that the dividend yield, compound interest, and share reinvestment in an appreciating stock eventually account for about 95 percent of the total return over time.

It amazes me how many investors buy a stock in the hope that its price will appreciate but give no regard to the dividend yield, one of the major factors in total return. I know the argument: Truly explosive-growth companies don't pay out their earnings in the form of a dividend; they reinvest them in their company so they can grow faster. But we aren't trying to gamble on which undiscovered company will be the next Wal-Mart. We just want to average double-digit returns and beat the pros, safely enough so we can spend our time on other things without worrying about our investments all the time.

Because the investing public invariably overreacts to even small, meaningless negative events in the press, a DJIA company's stock can decline for no good reason, driving its yields artificially high. It is in such periods when a company is undervalued that a buying opportunity is created. In the past, buying DJIA stocks cheap has resulted in large gains because these issues tend to bounce back up. They tend to be resilient and outgrow adverse news and corporate crises.

That, in a nutshell, is the key to the Top 10 strategy. You buy DJIA stocks when no one else wants them (when they're out of favor) and sell when the news is great and the world loves them and is willing to pay you a premium. In doing so, you're being a contrarian. Ironically, individual investors usually do just the opposite and wonder why they don't see good performance.

The Top 10 strategy eliminates all emotion from the stock-selection process. Its component parts are as follows:

1: Simply invest equal dollar amounts in each of the ten *highest-yielding* DJIA issues, and hold those stocks for one year.

2: After that one year, adjust your portfolio to reflect the new ten highest-yielding issues. This has averaged about three to four changes per year.

3: Repeat the process every year.

And that's it!

In case all these numbers are making your head spin, the following table offers some clarification:

ABC CORPORATION COMMON STOCK

Study closely the following illustration of three different price/yield scenarios: As price rises, yield decreases! / As price declines, yield increases!

Price per Share	Dividend per Share	Dividend Yield
$5	$1	20%
$10	$1	10%
$20	$1	5%

As you can see, *there is an inverse relationship between yield and price.* If, in our example, you bought ABC Corporation stock when it was a high "yielder," you'd have purchased it at $5 per share, based on its 20 percent yield. You'd be buying this out-of-favor issue at a deep discount. If the share price jumped back up to $20, equaling a 5 percent yield, the stock probably wouldn't appear on next year's high-yielding list. In that case, you'd sell it and trade it for another cheap, quality Dow company.

By choosing a portfolio of ten high-yield, low-price stocks, you're forced to buy low and sell high. In that way you avoid all guesswork in knowing when to buy and sell.

Why does this simple strategy work so well?

1. It forces you to buy out-of-favor stocks. "Buy low, sell high" is an old idea, but how many people really do it?
2. Once a year it recycles your money out of overvalued stocks and back into undervalued securities, based on yield. The discipline to sell is just as important, if not more so, as the decision to buy.
3. Yield! Owning stocks with above-average dividends gives you a major leg up on total returns.
4. The decision to buy and hold for twelve months avoids emotional reactions to the vagaries of the market.

Simple, right? But don't let the simplicity of this method fool you—the returns have been exceptional.

PERFORMANCE

How well has the yield on DJIA stocks identified value over the years? The Top 10 strategy has:

1. Outperformed the DJIA sixteen out of the last twenty-one years!
2. Had an annualized return of 16.58 percent for the last twenty-one years (since 1973). The Dow has had an annualized return of 11.04 percent for the same period. That's a total return 50 percent higher than the Dow itself!
3. Never lost money over any three-year market cycle.
4. Outperformed the DJIA in four of its five down years since 1973. It performs well in up *and* down markets.

As you can see from the opposite table, by using the Top 10 strategy your money would have increased more than twentyfold in

COMPARISON OF TOTAL RETURNS USING THE TOP 10 STRATEGY

Year	DHA Total Return	Total Value of a $10,000 Investment In the Dow 30 Made on Jan 1, 1973	Top 10 Total Return	Total Value of a $10,000 Investment in the Top 10 Made on Jan 1, 1973
1973	−13.12%	$8,688	−1.02%	$9,898
1974	−23.14	$6,678	−8.95	$9,012
1975	44.4	$9,643	56.73	$14,125
1976	22.72	$11,834	34.80	$19,041
1977	−12.7	$10,331	−0.83	$18,883
1978	2.69	$13,110	0.19	$18,919
1979	10.52	$14,489	12.38	$21,261
1980	21.41	$17,591	26.37	$26,868
1981	−3.40	$16,993	7.35	$28,843
1982	25.79	$21,376	25.46	$36,186
1983	25.68	$26,865	38.45	$50,100
1984	1.06	$28,477	6.89	$53,552
1985	32.78	$37,812	28.42	$68,772
1986	26.91	$47,987	29.87	$89,314
1987	6.02	$50,876	6.97	$95,298
1988	15.95	$58,991	21.60	$115,882
1989	31.71	$77,697	27.22	$147,425
1990	−0.57	$77,254	−7.94	$135,720
1991	23.93	$95,740	33.54	$181,241
1992	7.34	$102,767	8.26	$196,212
1993	8		18.17	
(1/93–6/93)		$110,988		$231,864
AVERAGE	11.04%		16.58%	

twenty-one years! And your end value is more than twice what it would have been had you invested in the Dow 30 stocks only.

Also, please note that all was not peachy at the beginning; had you adopted this method, you would have been down for the first two years. Many investors would have gotten discouraged with the strategy or whoever recommended it and would have pulled out. They would have gotten bored, given up, and missed out on years of powerful growth. Even though this chart doesn't consider inflation or transaction costs, you can see just how important an increase of a few percentage points can be in terms of return.

It's possible, by the way, to pursue the Top 10 strategy by means of something akin to a mutual fund, with all the advantages mutual funds provide (professional money management, automatic deposits, hassle-free paperwork, etc.). Most of the large brokerage firms offer a unit trust (similar to a mutual fund) that employs this strategy, and the charges are substantially lower than they'd be if you tried this on your own.

Now let's review how far we've come. Whereas you probably started this book with some misconceptions about what it takes to become wealthy, you now have a method for saving, a plan, and a low-risk, high-return investment strategy. Having thoroughly explored how to employ your resources effectively, let's talk finally about how you can direct them in a way that will demonstrate the level of your wealth and spirit.

PART 4

EVIDENCE OF MASTERY

WEALTH RITUAL 5

Act with Impact—
You've Got to Give to Live

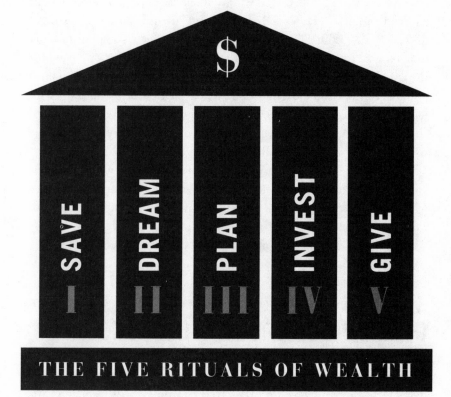

> **Gratitude is not only the greatest of all virtues, but the parent of all others.**
>
> —C I C E R O

WHILE ON VACATION IN DUBLIN, IRELAND, Henry Ford, the founder of the Ford Motor Company, was asked to contribute to a collection for a new orphanage. Judging the cause worthy, Ford promptly wrote out a check for £2,000. The next day the local papers covered the gift as headline news. However, the amount of the check was wrongly quoted as £20,000. The director of the orphanage visited Ford's hotel to apologize for the mistake, but Ford answered, "There's no need for that. I'll give you a check for the remaining eighteen thousand pounds, but only on one condition. When the new orphanage opens, I want a special inscription on it." The new building was erected shortly thereafter, and carved in stone above the entryway were the words: I WAS A STRANGER, AND YOU TOOK ME IN.

No matter how wealthy we become, I don't think we can ever be truly happy until we learn to use our economic power in a positive way for the benefit of others as well as ourselves. To enjoy our wealth fully and begin to use this free-flowing tool wisely, we must live by Wealth Ritual 5: **Act with impact. You've got to give to live!**

SAY YES: GIVE TO EVERYONE WHO ASKS

I have a simple rule that I live by: Give to everyone who asks. I firmly believe that our purpose in life is to try to make a difference in the lives of those around us. I believe in giving something back. Even if it's a simple gesture, I enjoy being able to play a part in doing something good. I've been so fortunate that I feel it's my duty to help others in need. Hence, I give something—no matter how small—to everyone who asks of me.

I'm sure you can think of many reasons to be grateful, to feel fortunate in your life. Try giving for a few weeks to everyone who

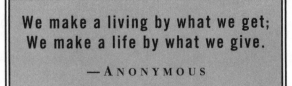

We make a living by what we get;
We make a life by what we give.

—ANONYMOUS

asks, and see if you don't feel better about yourself. See, too, if you don't notice others treating you with more generosity.

If you can't give people as much money or time as they want, do what you can. If you disagree with their cause, at least give them a kind word.

BE A TWO-QUARTER PERSON

Mahatma Gandhi, India's late spiritual leader, stepped aboard a train one day. As he did, one of his shoes slipped off and landed on the track. Immediately a beggar picked it up and began to run. To his companions' amazement, Gandhi calmly took off his other shoe and tossed it onto the tracks near the beggar. "Now the poor man will have a pair he can use," he said.

I don't know where I first heard about being a two-quarter person, but I like it. It means that if someone asks you for a quarter, you give them two. Without fail, you try to give more than is expected of you. It's fun. Especially if you do it out of real compassion, rather than obligation. Believe me, it will change the way you think about yourself and your money.

If you have trouble giving, if you feel it's just too scary, be patient and don't worry. It's new and you'll feel a bit uncomfortable for a while. I've heard it said that once we begin to understand our own limitations, we can begin to have compassion for others. If you have trouble letting go of those greenbacks, realize that you have a limitation that is keeping you from experiencing the level of joy you deserve to get from your money. Once you understand this, it'll get easier.

Even if you're already a cheerful giver, understand that you may need to ease into the role of being a two-quarter person. That's okay,

> **Don't let your possessions possess you.**
>
> —H. JACKSON BROWNE

just make sure you're improving every day in your generosity. Legendary basketball coach John Wooden said it best: "You can't have a perfect day without doing something for someone who'll never be able to repay you."

Let me offer another suggestion. We've talked a great deal about beliefs and rituals and about how important it is to have a wealthy mind-set. It's apparent that everything is really created twice: first in thought, then in realization. It follows that to experience wealth on a grand scale, we have to think like wealthy people. We can't just *do*— that's not enough in the long term. We must *become*. We have to become wealthy in thought and action.

Too many people approach being a giver from the wrong perspective. They look at the resources they possess and invariably fail to see any "extra" they can part with. That's wrongheaded thinking. Remember: *If you don't feel secure enough to give, you'll never feel wealthy at the deepest level.*

I once interviewed an extremely successful businesswoman in my community. Her name is Ninfa Laurenzo, founder of Ninfa's Mexican Cafe restaurant chain. Ninfa started her business in her late forties with nothing but her love of cooking, a belief in herself, and a deep faith in God. She brought the pots and pans from her own kitchen to serve her first professional meal. Today she moves in circles that include former presidents, celebrities, and notable business leaders.

But as impressive as her business success is, her generosity is even more impressive. Of all the comments Ninfa made to me in that interview, there's one I find particularly memorable. We were discussing giving and contribution, and the fact that she'd once spent a small fortune on billboards that said only GRACIAS as her way of thanking a country that had rewarded her efforts so miraculously. I asked her exactly when she had gotten her passion for helping others. She was surprised by my question, but without hesitation, she said, "Start? Well, we've always given. That's just our nature. We gave and gave and gave, even when we didn't have it."

When someone like Mama Ninfa—the name given to her by her family, friends, and even brief acquaintances—says, "even when we didn't have it," you can be certain that we're talking about a level of generosity and love that is deeper than most people would dare stretch. When Ninfa didn't have any money to give, she gave food made with her own hands. Even if she didn't own a successful business, I would consider Mama Ninfa wealthy by anyone's standards because she knows how to give. That's the secret to living abundantly.

A remarkable phenomenon I've observed is that once we give enough of ourself, our brain suddenly gets the message that there's enough to go around. Something clicks, and we feel like we can take care of our own needs and help others too. I can't tell you the exact dollar contribution that will produce this mind-set, but I will say this: *Don't cheat yourself by holding back.*

You can't give just a tiny bit and sit back, waiting for your ship to come in. You have to give with selflessness. And, if you don't feel like you can, then you *must*. It's the only way you can break free. We've already established how wealthy you really are, regardless of your situation. You know that you're wealthier than the majority of the world. You have to ask yourself: How rich is rich? How much is enough? How wealthy will I have to be before I become a good steward?

You know the answer: *It all starts in the belief that you're wealthy right now.*

A WORTHWHILE CAUSE

Every business day, on my short walk from the parking lot to my office, I walk right through the homestead of a man named Bill. Bill is homeless. He roams the streets of downtown Houston, but he's always on this certain corner at 7:00 A.M. Perhaps he feels comfortable seeing the same people pass him every day—maybe it makes him feel like he's part of something or some organization. I don't know. However, I know that Bill is not mentally stable because he never remembers me, even though I give him money every single day.

Bill's easy to spot: He's in his midforties, overweight, unshaven and unbathed, with shaggy hair, mismatched shoes, and overalls with no shirt underneath during the summer months. He's not threatening in the least and seems like a very gentle soul. He doesn't talk much—perhaps because he feels like nobody cares what he has to say.

Unfortunately, he is probably right. In fact, many people wish he would just disappear off the face of the planet. I don't know why I stopped to introduce myself to him one day almost two years ago. He just intrigued me. He doesn't seem mean, or criminal—just lost. I can see under his unshaven face a person who is dying to be somebody—to be recognized as a person. He could be somebody's father. At times, I wonder who his parents are and whether he's ever had any other life, besides the street. I bet he has an interesting, albeit painful, story that we could learn something from.

What makes me especially sad, looking at Bill, is that in this country there are an estimated two to three million people living on the streets, with the fastest-growing segment of the homeless population being women and children. If you're looking for a way to contribute, helping the homeless would be an extremely worthy cause to support. You could:

- Lead food drives
- Tutor
- Get your business involved
- Recycle household necessities
- Employ the homeless
- Organize clothing drives
- Volunteer at a shelter
- Provide child care
- Work politically to create affordable housing and support solutions to the many indirect causes of homelessness: poverty, poor education, joblessness, substance abuse, etc.

Charitable organizations that can make particularly good use of your resources and talents include:

The National Alliance to End Homelessness, (202) 638-1526
American Red Cross, National Headquarters, (202) 639-3610
The United Way of America, (703) 836-7100
The Salvation Army, (201) 239-0606

Let me leave this subject of giving with a wonderful story about Alexander the Great. Although he conquered Persia and annexed it for Macedonia, Alexander III had a generous heart. Before a military journey to Asia he became concerned about the finances of his soldiers. He knew they wouldn't be able to provide for their families while they were away. To ease their burden and help feed his constituents, he distributed his entire kingdom, crown estates, and revenues among their dependents. When the royal resources were depleted, his friend asked Alexander what he'd reserved for himself. Solemnly, the king answered, "Hope. All I have reserved for myself is hope, but hope is more than enough."

TYING IT ALL TOGETHER

Obtaining financial freedom, whether it be in America or any other country, is relatively simple: Earn an income, seek your own personal form of excellence, and learn to save and invest properly. Anybody can become wealthy if he lets patience, discipline, time, and the free enterprise system become his allies.

Over the course of this book I've tried to indoctrinate you in the basic habits necessary to create and sustain wealth:

- Save a portion of your income (at least 10 percent) for yourself, even if you have to pay yourself first.
- Make sure you're living within your means, even if you have to develop a budget.
- Continually look for ways to expand who you are and the level of service you provide.
- Seek your dreams and the financial success that follows.
- Always have a financial plan in place; before you can hit a target you must decide on one.
- Invest in the free enterprise system by choosing a diversified portfolio of common stocks (preferably using the Top 10 strategy), and let time work for you.
- Make sure you use your wealth in a constructive way by contributing to a worthwhile cause.
- Finally, continue to develop and strengthen the wealthy habits that will support you throughout your lifetime.

Use the following summary and checklist to tie it all together.

THE FIVE RITUALS OF WEALTH

Summary and Checklist

1. PRACTICE: Pay yourself first.
   BELIEF: It's okay to keep some.
   PURPOSE: Become a saver.
   QUESTION: Ask yourself, Where am I now in terms of managing the financial resources I already possess?
   IMMEDIATE ACTION: Begin or continue to set aside no less than 10 percent of your earnings in savings.

2. PRACTICE: Seek your dream!
   BELIEF: If you do what you love, the money will follow.
   PURPOSE: Create your own worthwhile form of self-expression.
   QUESTION: Ask yourself, How can I fulfill my ultimate purpose and create wealth in the process?
   IMMEDIATE ACTION: Define in detail and begin to work actively toward your lifework and ultimate vision.

3. PRACTICE: Maintain a plan.
   BELIEF: The map becomes the territory.
   PURPOSE: Become a planner/goal setter/financial achiever.
   QUESTION: Ask yourself, Where do I want to go financially (in five years, ten years, my lifetime)?
   IMMEDIATE ACTION: Develop and maintain a financial plan that includes all major goals.

4. PRACTICE: Employ your resources.
   BELIEF: Money goes where it's treated best.
   PURPOSE: Become a long-term passive investor.
   QUESTION: Ask yourself, How do I best reach my financial goals?
   IMMEDIATE ACTION: Start and continue your passive

investment program, preferably using the Top 10
strategy.

5. **PRACTICE:** Act with impact.
   BELIEF: You've got to give to live.
   PURPOSE: Become a giver.
   QUESTION: Ask yourself, In what ways can I use my
   wealth for the positive benefit of myself and
   others?
   IMMEDIATE ACTION: Find and consistently contribute to a
   worthwhile cause (work toward 10 percent).

A TIME FOR ACTION

Nothing in this world is as powerful as an individual choosing to take
action. Decisions shape our future and our destiny. Not making decisions does the same. These rituals of wealth are timeless. They're not
complicated, but their application on a habitual basis is a challenge.
My final request of you is this: Write down the pros and cons of
beginning a program like this. And if it makes sense, do something
about it. Make the decision to go for your dreams while you have all
of the facts at your fingertips.

If it doesn't make sense, don't do it. But please don't rob yourself
of the opportunity to get your financial future immediately in order
because you failed to make a decision. I realized a long time ago that
decision makers are the ones who have the power in America—
they're the successful ones, the ones we emulate.

*People who can't make decisions because they're scared of mak-
ing a mistake are the ones whose progress is perpetually stalled.*

Could you make a mistake? Could you decide to set aside 10 percent of your income for your estate and find it somewhat uncomfortable at first? Could you make an investment and lose some money?
The answer to these two questions is, of course, yes. But by making
the decision to do nothing, you know that eventually you'll lose
everything. The only way to have a shot at your dreams is to make a
decision to act.

> Two roads diverged
> in a wood, and I—
> I took the one less traveled by,
> And that has made
> all the difference.
>
> —ROBERT FROST

Henry David Thoreau once wrote, "The mass of men lead lives of quiet desperation." This is true of far too many people in this world, people who've let fear stand in the way of their hopes and dreams. Realize that fear is part of the growing process, especially in the world of investments. Currency devaluates, tax laws change, governments rise and fall, companies prosper and fail, people change, and through it all, life goes on. Any quest for absolute security is a waste of time because our world is designed for constant and continuous change.

Given the circumstances in which we find ourselves at this point in history, I say: *Go for it!* Don't settle for less than you can be financially. Remember that life is to be lived, and that action cures fear.

May you be wealthy always!

EXHIBIT 1: MONTHLY EXPENSE ORGANIZER

		JAN.	FEB.	MAR.	APR.	MAY	JUNE	JULY	AUG.	SEP.	OCT.	NOV.	DEC.
Monthly Income (after deductions)													
Expense Categories	Budget												
Total Monthly Expenses													
Monthly Balance													

EXHIBIT 2: DAILY EXPENSE FORM

DATE	AMOUNT	CATEGORY	TYPE	PRIORITY

PRIORITIES: A- Necessary, B- Important, C- Nice, D- Worthless

EXHIBIT 3:
PARTIAL DEDUCTIONS: IRA

FILING SINGLE	FILING JOINTLY	MAXIMUM TAXABLE DEDUCTION
Income up to $25,000	Income up to $40,000	$2,000 (per acount)
26,000	41,000	1,800
27,000	42,000	1,600
28,000	43,000	1,400
29,000	44,000	1,200
30,000	45,000	1,000
31,000	46,000	800
32,000	47,000	600
33,000	48,000	400
34,000	49,000	200
35,000+	50,000+	0

EXHIBIT 4: $1 PRINCIPAL COMPOUNDED ANNUALLY

END OF YEAR	3%	5%	8%	10%	12%	15%
1	1.0300	1.0500	1.0800	1.1000	1.1200	1.1500
2	1.0609	1.1025	1.1664	1.2100	1.2544	1.3225
3	1.0927	1.1576	1.2597	1.3310	1.4049	1.5209
4	1.1255	1.2155	1.3605	1.4641	1.5735	1.7490
5	1.1593	1.2763	1.4693	1.6105	1.7623	2.0114
6	1.1941	1.3401	1.5869	1.7716	1.9738	2.3131
7	1.2299	1.4071	1.7138	1.9487	2.2107	2.6600
8	1.2668	1.4775	1.8509	2.1436	2.4760	3.0590
9	1.3048	1.5513	1.9990	2.3579	2.7731	3.5179
10	1.3439	1.6289	2.1589	2.5937	3.1058	4.0456
11	1.3842	1.7103	2.3316	2.8531	3.4785	4.6524
12	1.4258	1.7959	2.5182	3.1384	3.8960	5.3503
13	1.4685	1.8856	2.7196	3.4523	4.3635	6.1528
14	1.5126	1.9799	2.9372	3.7975	4.8871	7.0757
15	1.5580	2.0789	3.1722	4.1772	5.4736	8.1371
16	1.6047	2.1829	3.4259	4.5950	6.1304	9.3576
17	1.6528	2.2920	3.7000	5.0545	6.8660	10.7613
18	1.7024	2.4066	3.9960	5.5599	7.6900	12.3755
19	1.7535	2.5270	4.3157	6.1159	8.6128	14.2318
20	1.8061	2.6533	4.6610	6.7275	9.6463	16.3665
21	1.8603	2.7860	5.0338	7.4002	10.8038	18.8215
22	1.9161	2.9253	5.4365	8.1403	12.1003	21.6447
23	1.9736	3.0715	5.8715	8.9543	13.5523	24.8915
24	2.0328	3.2251	6.3412	9.8497	15.1786	28.6252
25	2.0938	3.3864	6.8485	10.8347	17.0001	32.9190
26	2.1566	3.5557	7.3964	11.9182	19.0401	37.8568
27	2.2213	3.7335	7.9881	13.1100	21.3249	43.5353
28	2.2879	3.9201	8.6271	14.4210	23.8839	50.0656
29	2.3566	4.1161	9.3173	15.8631	26.7499	57.5755

END OF YEAR	3%	5%	8%	10%	12%	15%
30	2.4273	4.3219	10.0627	17.4494	29.9599	66.2118
31	2.5001	4.5380	10.8677	19.1943	33.5551	76.1435
32	2.5751	4.7649	11.7371	21.1138	37.5817	87.5651
33	2.6523	5.0032	12.6760	23.2252	42.0915	100.6998
34	2.7319	5.2533	13.6901	25.5477	47.1425	115.8048
35	2.8139	5.5160	14.7853	28.1024	52.7996	133.1755
36	2.8983	5.7918	15.9682	30.9127	59.1356	153.1519
37	2.9852	6.0814	17.2456	34.0039	66.2318	176.1246
38	3.0748	6.3855	18.6253	37.4043	74.1797	202.5433
39	3.1670	6.7048	20.1153	41.1448	83.0812	232.9248
40	3.2620	7.0400	21.7245	45.2593	93.0510	267.8635

SUGGESTED READING

Ailes, Roger. *You Are the Message.*

Allen, James. *As a Man Thinketh.*

Blanchard, Ken. *Raving Fans.*

Boldt, Lawrence G. *Zen and the Art of Making a Living.*

Chilton, David. *The Wealthy Barber.*

Clason, George S. *The Richest Man in Babylon.*

Covey, Stephen. *The Seven Habits of Highly Effective People.*

Dyer, Wayne. *Real Magic.*

Frankl, Victor E. *Man's Search for Meaning.*

Franklin, Benjamin. *The Way to Wealth.*

Hill, Napoleon. *Think and Grow Rich.*

Johnson, Spencer. *The One-Minute Salesperson.*

Laut, Phil. *Money Is My Friend.*

Leonard, George. *Mastery.*

O'Higgins, Michael. *Beating the Dow.*

Robbins, Anthony. *Unlimited Power.*

Robbins, Anthony. *Awaken the Giant Within.*

Roger and McWilliams. *Wealth 101.*

Sinetar, Marsha. *Do What You Love, the Money Will Follow.*

Underwood and Brown. *Grow Rich Slowly: The Merrill Lynch Guide to Retirement Planning,*